The Making of the Potterverse

The
Making of the
Potterverse

A Month-by-Month Look at Harry's First 10 Years

SCOTT THOMAS

ECW Press

Copyright © Scott Thomas, 2007

Published by ECW PRESS
2120 Queen Street East, Suite 200, Toronto, Ontario, Canada M4E 1E2

LIBRARY AND ARCHIVES CANADA CATALOGUING IN PUBLICATION
Scott Thomas
The making of the Potterverse :
a month-by-month look at Harry's first 10 years / Scott Thomas.

ISBN-13: 978-1-55022-763-5
ISBN-10: 1-55022-763-7

1. Rowling, J. K.—Criticism and interpretation.
2. Rowling, J.K.—Characters—Harry Potter.
3. Children's stories, English—History and criticism.
4. Fantasy fiction, English—History and criticism.
5. Potter, Harry (Fictitious character) I. Title.

PR6068.O94Z65 2007   823'.914   C2006-906904-2

Developing editor: Jennifer Hale
Cover and text design: Tania Craan
Typesetting: Gail Nina
Printed by Transcontinental

DISTRIBUTION

CANADA: Jaguar Book Group, 100 Armstrong Avenue, Georgetown, on, L7G 5S4
UNITED STATES: Independent Publishers Group, 814 North Franklin Street,
Chicago, Illinois 60610

PRINTED AND BOUND IN CANADA

ECW PRESS
ecwpress.com

*To my wife, Eileen, who keeps the
magic alive in our relationship.*

The Making of the Potterverse

AN INTRODUCTION

In 1992, Harry Potter was the son of a World War II bomber pilot who was being honored posthumously.

Two years after that, he was an accountant.

And two years after *that*, he found himself serving Texas as Assistant Attorney General.

No disrespect intended to those Harry Potters, but their accomplishments, big or small, simply can't compare to the Harry Potter who was born 10 years ago as the lead character of J.K. Rowling's first published work of fiction — *Harry Potter and the Philosopher's Stone*. *That* Harry Potter captured the imagination of the world, changed the fate of his creator and made stockholders in numerous publishing companies and one Hollywood studio *very* happy.

Ten years on it's difficult to imagine a time when Harry Potter, Hermione Granger, Ron Weasley and Hogwarts School of Witchcraft and Wizardry weren't in the popular vernacular. There was, indeed, a pre-Harry world; it just wasn't as much fun.

In under a decade, Rowling has joined such literary luminaries as Lewis Carroll, L. Frank Baum, J.R.R. Tolkien and Roald Dahl, and created a realm that is every bit as fanciful as theirs, whether it be Wonderland, Oz, Middle Earth or Willy Wonka's chocolate factory. And, most importantly, the audience has completely fallen in love with that realm, embracing each novel as it is published as well as each movie adaptation, and elevating Rowling herself to the literary equivalent of a rock star. But maybe her success isn't all that surprising when you consider her background and the journey she's been on from destitute single mother to billionaire author. Rowling's creative spirit has touched the heart of the global audience in a way that few authors have been able to, and her life story, in itself, is a tale as magical as anything Harry has been through.

If you have any doubts, just consider the way in which Harry was created. "I had the idea for Harry on a train in the summer of 1990," she explained. In fact, she has described the scene in a number of interviews. "I was sitting on the train. I was staring out the window. As far as I can remember, I was staring at some cows — not the most inspiring subject — and the idea just came. I cannot tell you why or what happened to trigger it. It was the purest stroke of inspiration I've ever had. And I'd been writing for years and never tried to get anything published. Harry came pretty much fully formed. I saw him very clearly. I could see this skinny little boy with black hair, this weird scar on his forehead. I knew instantly that he was a wizard, but he didn't know that yet. Then I began to work out his background. That was the basic idea. I didn't know then that it was going to be a book for children. I just knew that I had this boy, Harry. During the [train] journey I also discovered Ron, Nearly Headless Nick, Hagrid and Peeves. But with the idea of my life careening round my head, I didn't have a pen that worked. And I never went anywhere without my pen and notebook. So, rather than trying to write it, I had to think it. And I think that was a very good thing. I was besieged by a mass of detail and if it didn't survive that journey, it probably wasn't worth remembering.

"When I was younger, I think my greatest fantasy would have been to find out that I had powers that I'd never dreamt of. That I was special. That 'these people couldn't be my parents, I'm far more interesting than that.' I think a lot of children might have secretly thought that sometimes. So I just took that one stage further and I thought, 'What's the best way of breaking free of that? Okay, you're magic.'"

And so is the entire Harry Potter phenomenon; a phenomenon that we celebrate in *The Making of the Potterverse*, bringing you through a decade of Harry-related headlines, month by month and year by year. In that period, the world has changed in so many ways and not all for the better, but Harry Potter and the work of J.K. Rowling serve as an escape when our reality gets too overwhelming, offering friends we can count on to do what's right and touching us with a little bit of magic. And you can never have too much magic.

— Scott Thomas

Spring 1997

In an article that begins with the words "A young author has sold her first book to an American publisher for more than 100,000 pounds," J.K. Rowling was introduced to the world thanks to a piece in the *Telegraph*. Like most of the articles of the time, it detailed that Rowling was a single mother who wrote as often as she could, relied for a time on public assistance and then, some would say miraculously, made her sale. In describing Harry's adventures, the journalist noted, "It tells the story of Harry Potter, an orphan who thinks he is an ordinary boy, brought up by a cruel uncle and aunt. He discovers that he is a wizard and, as in C.S. Lewis' Narnia series, he passes through a time warp into a world of make-believe. Encouraged by her success, Miss Rowling plans a further six books recounting the adventures of Harry Potter." The book, titled *Harry Potter and the Philosopher's Stone*, was published on June 26, 1997, in the United Kingdom.

Producer David Heyman caught wind of Harry Potter at about this time. As he explained, he had had started his company, Heyman Films, with the intention of producing films that would be appropriate for his brother and sister, who were 10 and 14 at the time. "My Head of Development, Tanya Seghatchian, read an article about a new children's book by a then-unknown author," he explained. "The agent sent her a copy and my assistant Nisha read it over the weekend. Nisha reported that it was a curious book about a young boy who goes to wizard school. I thought it was a wonderful idea and read the novel that evening. What I thought was a great idea turned out to be an even more remarkable book, and so much

J.K. Rowling (Louis M. Lanzano/AP Photo)

richer than the idea that initially attracted me. I realized this was something very special and began pursuing the rights the following morning." He added that when he met J.K. Rowling, "I made her a promise to be true to her vision. This was and has been the most important consideration to me throughout the process. I told her how I wanted to keep the darkness and the edge of the material intact. I also think Jo was excited by the fact that I wanted her to be involved in the creative process. And she was an invaluable collaborator. Her inspiration and ideas were absolutely wonderful."

Summer 1997

The *Herald* in Glasgow offered a profile of Rowling, elaborating on her background, her struggles and her efforts to sell Harry Potter. In the course of the interview, Rowling admitted, "This book saved my sanity. Apart from my sister, I knew nobody. I've never been more broke and the little I had saved went on baby gear. In the wake of my marriage [ending], having worked all my life, I was suddenly an unemployed single parent in a grotty little flat. The manuscript was the only thing I had going for me." A number of other publications provided more details of her past and the initial development of Harry Potter, among them: the *Sunday Times*, the *Scotsman*, and the *Electronic Telegraph*.

The manuscript for *Harry Potter and the Philosopher's Stone* (renamed *Harry Potter and the Sorcerer's Stone* in America) had been completed in 1996, and attracted the attention of agent Christopher Little, who wanted to represent J.K. Rowling. Eight UK publishers ultimately rejected the manuscript, but Bloomsbury took it on, offering the author a $4,000 advance.

When the first Harry Potter went into auction in America, Scholastic managed to secure the rights for about $100,000 — an unbelievable amount as far as J.K. Rowling was concerned (and, ironically, about one percent of what she's worth in 2007). In addition, the *Bristol Evening Post* reported that two Hollywood studios were attempting to secure a deal for the films based on the rights David Heyman had acquired.

November 1997

·······················

Following the sale of *Harry Potter and the Philosopher's Stone*, Rowling took home, in her mind, an even bigger prize: a gold medal and £2,500 as part of the Nestlé Smarties Book Prize — the children's equivalent of The Booker. "It's a particularly wonderful award to win from my point of view," she told the press, "because the final judging is done by children and they are obviously the people whose opinions matter to me the most." She also mentioned that she planned on a seven-book series and that she was halfway through book three, having already finished book two, *Harry Potter and the Chamber of Secrets*. Most surprisingly, she added, "I also have another children's book half-finished." No further word on *that* particular project.

March 1998

Nestlé Smarties winner J.K. Rowling visited the school she used to attend, the Forest of Dean, where she talked to students about becoming a writer and encouraged them to read. At the time, the press noted that the first Harry novel had sold 35,000 copies.

April 1998

The "good humor and pace" of the first Harry Potter novel got it into the top four of the *Guardian*'s Children's Fiction Prize.

May 1998

The Scottish Braille Press made a Braille edition of *Harry Potter and the Philosopher's Stone*. Sally McCallum of the Braille Press said, "Everyone was really excited about publishing *Harry Potter* in Braille because the book was so good and it is important to have good books in Braille for children." Added author J.K. Rowling, "It is wonderful. I'm really honored that the title has been chosen."

June 1998

J.K. Rowling paid a surprise visit to Alford Primary School in England, where she read from her novels and took questions from the students.

July 1998

The *Electronic Telegraph* conducted an interview with Rowling and in the accompanying profile observed, "When her first novel was published last year, Rowling became a literary sensation. The novel won her the Smarties Prize — the children's equivalent of the Booker. It was sold to eight other countries, netting a $100,000 advance for the American edition, a huge sum for a first novel, almost unheard of for a children's novel. Such is the excitement about Joanne Rowling that she is being compared to C.S. Lewis and Roald Dahl, who also achieved the rare trick of delighting both children and adults. The secret seems to be that her target [audience] consists of one person: herself." This article was also the first mention of a possible Harry Potter film deal, though Rowling couldn't really comment on it at that early juncture.

Harry Potter and the Chamber of Secrets was published in Britain. Of the book's arrival in the UK, The *Scotsman* wrote, "The second novel, *Harry Potter and the Chamber of Secrets*, has leapt to the top of the hardback bestseller lists, overtaking adult works with all the élan of a gracefully speeding broomstick. Certainly, young readers have been clamoring for the next installment of Harry's funny, scary, magical life. It is the book which will keep the beloved offspring quiet for substantial segments of the summer holidays. Yet adults, not all of them teachers or parents avidly curious to learn what has so enthralled their children, are it seems almost equally allured by Harry's escapades at Hogwarts. This is as it should be. The great children's books have always transcended petty boundaries of age."

August 1998

The value of Bloomsbury stock was being driven upward by the success of J.K. Rowling's creation.

September 1998

The *Irish Times* offered a story that expressed amazement at the success of the Harry Potter novels, noting in particular that they had knocked John Grisham from the top of the bestseller lists.

In reviewing *Harry Potter and the Sorcerer's Stone*, *Booklist* opined, "Rowling's first novel, which has won numerous prizes in England,

So many tourists have come to King's Cross station in London looking for Platform 9¾, the station management decided to erect a sign. (Fionna Boyle)

is a brilliantly imagined and beautifully written fantasy that incorporates elements of traditional British school stories without once violating the magical underpinnings of the plot. In fact, Rowling's wonderful ability to put a fantastic spin on sports, student rivalry, and eccentric faculty contributes to the humor, charm, and, well, delight of her utterly captivating story." Added the *Columbus Dispatch*, "Published last year in Great Britain and released just this month in the United States, the novel blends a rollicking adventure with supernatural inventions and themes of courage and home. Compared by English reviewers to Roald Dahl fantasies, the novel does indeed bear similarities: flamboyant characters clearly divided into camps of good and evil, an unsqueamish embrace of sorcery, and empowered children who nevertheless remain childlike."

October 1998

Heyday Films (David Heyman's company) officially announced its acquisition of the film rights to the Harry Potter novels, with Warner Brothers as official distributors. Said Rowling, "I am in a kind of stunned relief. The talks went on for months and months and at some stages I thought it would never happen. It will be an incredible experience to see in real life what I have seen inside my mind. It will be quite disorientating, but wonderful."

Bloomsbury expected sales of Harry Potter novels to exceed 300,000 by the end of the year.

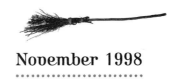

November 1998

The AP conducted an interview with Rowling in which she made an interesting comment about the creative process: "I have a very visual imagination. I see it, then I try to describe what is in my mind's eye," she said.

December 1998

Early in the month, J.K. Rowling sat for an in-depth interview with National Public Radio.

In a short profile of Rowling, *Newsweek* wrote, "Rowling's Cinderella-like story began eight years ago in Edinburgh. An unemployed schoolteacher and the divorced mother of a three-month-old daughter, she began to write out of desperation, convinced that she had nothing left to lose. To escape her chilly flat, she wheeled her daughter's stroller through the streets until the baby fell asleep. Then she would dash into a coffee shop and write. Unable to afford either a word processor or the cost of copying her manuscript, she typed it out twice and sent it off to publishers. The day her English publisher bought the story, she says, was 'comparable only to having my daughter.'"

January 1999

Rowling took part in an online chat hosted by Amazon.co.uk. In that interview she pointed out that, "My first two novels — which I never tried to get published — were for adults. I suppose I might write another one, but I never really imagine a target audience when I'm writing. The ideas come first, so it really depends on the idea that grabs me next."

The months that followed brought many interviews with J.K. Rowling in which she detailed aspects of the process of creation, such as how the idea for Harry Potter had come to her while riding on a train; the development of certain characters; her struggles as a single mother and the financial desperation she was living through; and the fact that even at this early stage of her success, her life was definitely on an upward swing. The indication was also that she simply had no idea how successful she and her creation would ultimately become.

June 1999

Harry Potter and the Chamber of Secrets was published on June 2, debuting at the #1 position on several charts, and the publisher quickly moved 700,000 copies. *Entertainment Weekly* reported,

"Originally scheduled for fall '99, *Chamber of Secrets* was rushed out three months early because Scholastic was horrified by the flood of Internet sales of the British edition." For this same reason, Scholastic announced that they would be publishing book three, *Harry Potter and the Prisoner of Azkaban*, in the near future, only a few weeks after its British publication. *Entertainment Weekly* speculated, "Some publishing insiders believe the series may spur big changes in the industry: Rights to popular authors may soon be sold by language instead of by country."

August 1999

While appearing on Britain's Radio 4's Book Club series, J.K. Rowling was asked her opinion of why Harry Potter had taken off the way he had, with host James Naughtie noting, "Nothing like this has happened in children's literature for quite a long time." Said Rowling, "I always find it very hard to talk about the book in these terms, because I find it very, very difficult to be objective about them. To me, they remain my private little world. I was writing about Harry for five years before anyone else read a word of him and it's still an amazing feeling to me to be in a room, as we are today, with people whose heads are also populated with these characters, because, as I say, for five years, they were my private secret. From the moment I had the idea for the book, I could see a lot of comic potential in the idea that wizards walk among us and that we are foolishly blind to the fact that the reason that we keep losing our keys is that wizards are bewitching them for fun.

September 1999

A foreshadowing of things to come occurred when CNN reported on an Atlanta, Georgia, bookstore that opened up early to accommodate Harry Potter fans who had gathered beforehand to acquire copies of *The Prisoner of Azkaban*. By the release of book four, *Harry Potter and the Goblet of Fire*, this would be nothing by comparison.

In an interview with *Time* magazine, J.K. Rowling admitted that a regular character would probably perish in the next novel. "I am writing about someone, Voldemort, who is evil," she said. "The only way to show how evil he is is to take a life, to kill someone the reader really cares about."

Word leaked out that Warner Brothers had apparently snapped up the rights to the Harry Potter novels in a seven-figure deal, which one newspaper referred to as "a shocking amount for a 'kids' movie." The report also noted: "Rowling says that she intends to make the tone of the books darker and scarier as the boy wizard and his friends age. All the prospective directors have made movies dealing with the fantastic and the dark."

Appearing on CBS's *60 Minutes*, J.K. Rowling was asked by reporter Lesley Stahl how long she had been developing Harry. According to the author it had been for quite some time. "What amused me — I went through this last night to show you — this is my employment history [she holds up a series of papers]. [Harry material] is on the back of stuff that I really should have been doing at work, and on the front you have bits of my writing. This is really old.

This is a photocopy from a textbook when I was teaching in Portugal. And obviously this was what I was supposed to be doing with the children, and on the back you've got all the ghosts for Gryffindor."

October 1999

A South Carolina mom made headlines when she called for the Harry novels to be banned due to the fact that they carry a tone of "sheer evil." Rowling said, "I don't pretend that an evil presence is a cardboard cutout and nobody gets hurt."

Back in 1964, the Beatles had five spots in America's Top 10 singles. It seems that Harry Potter was giving them a bit of a run for their money when, shortly after the publication of *Prisoner of Azkaban*, J.K. Rowling's novels held the top three slots in the country's bestseller lists.

While on her North America tour to promote book three, Rowling visited students at a Montclair, New Jersey, school. There she read excerpts and took questions from the students.

A bookstore signing in Worcester, Massachusetts, drew thousands of fans. Larry J. Abramoff, owner of Tatnuck Bookseller, observed, "We're absolutely overwhelmed by the turnout. We couldn't believe that people were arriving so early." They began arriving at 11 a.m., some with lawn chairs and picnic baskets. Rowling wasn't scheduled to arrive until 7 p.m. The pattern of unprecedented crowds continued at every bookstore she went to.

December 1999

Rowling won her third consecutive Smarties Prize, this time for *Azkaban*. Grateful for the award that was voted on by 200 separate groups of children, she nonetheless announced, as reported by the BBC, that she didn't think future Harry novels should be nominated. Said Rowling at the British-based ceremony, "Believe it or not, third time round means the most to me, it really does. Two years ago when Harry wasn't famous at all he won the Smarties Award and it was the first thing Harry ever won. In fact, it was the first thing I won in my life, ever, apart from a book about how to grow potted plants. But I feel now in writing this series, and after this award, that Harry should not be submitted from now on for the Smarties Award."

The respect for Rowling's work continued as she was credited by the Boarding Education Alliance for helping to recreate the image for boarding schools. Ann Williamson of the BEA said, "The books have probably done more for boarding than anything else we could have imagined."

People magazine proclaimed J.K. Rowling to be one of the 24 Most Intriguing People of 1999.

Three young wizards read the Canadian edition of Harry Potter and the
Prisoner of Azkaban. *(Fred Lum/CP Photo)*

January 2000

Salon.com offered a critical examination of the Harry novels,
focusing on the fact that in Rowling's universe the boys definitely
finish first. "Harry's fictional realm of magic and wizardry perfectly
mirrors the conventional assumption that men do and should run
the world," opined writer Christine Schoefer. "From the beginning
of the first Potter book, it is boys and men, wizards and sorcerers
who catch our attention by dominating the scenes and determining
the action. . . . It is easy to see why boys love Harry's adventures.
And I know that girls' uncanny ability to imagine themselves in
male roles enables them to dissociate from the limitations of female
characters. But I wonder about the parents, many of whom join
their kids in reading the Harry Potter stories. Is our longing for a
magical world so deep, our hunger to be surprised and amazed so
intense, our gratitude for a well-told story so great that we are

willing to abdicate our critical judgment? Or are the stereotypes in the story integral to our fascination — do we feel comforted by a world in which conventional roles are firmly in place?"

It was announced that two new Harry Potter–related books were on the way: *Fantastic Beasts and Where to Find Them* and *Quidditch through the Ages*. "I have always had a hankering to write these two books," J.K. Rowling related, describing them as short stories that would each contain illustrations done by the author.

Around the middle of the month, word had really begun heating up regarding a potential Harry Potter feature film (for which Warner Brothers had snapped up the rights). Several directorial names were bandied around, though it seemed likely that Steven Spielberg would be the one to take on the project. Considering his track record — including *Close Encounters*, *E.T.* and the Indiana Jones films — the news was hardly surprising.

February 2000

J.K. Rowling took home the Author of the Year Award at the 11th annual British Book Awards, beating out such competitors as Stephen King, Colin Dexter and Terry Pratchett. It wasn't all good news, however, as Nancy Stouffer, an author from Camp Hill, Pennsylvania, filed a lawsuit claiming that Rowling had stolen elements of her 1984 novel, *The Legend of Rah and the Muggles*, in creating Harry Potter. A Scholastic spokeswoman explained, "Unfortunately, success often leads to frivolous claims, and we're confident the court will find in our favor."

Apparently Steven Spielberg's involvement with the first Harry Potter film was much more than just a series of rumors. Toward the end of the month, he issued a statement that basically said he would *not* be directing. "I have every certainty that the series of Harry Potter movies will be phenomenally successful," he said. "J.K. Rowling's vision of Harry Potter is modern genius. Warner Brothers and [studio president] Alan Horn have been more than generous in the time they've allowed me to make a decision. However, at this time, my directorial interests are taking me in another direction. Most importantly, I look forward to reading the fourth Harry Potter book this summer and taking my family to see the first movie."

March 2000

Volunteers looking to raise money for England's Oxfam charity bookshops went through the inventory of said stores looking for seemingly worthless donated books, hoping to find some gems among them. The search paid off with about 300 novels that turned to be quite valuable indeed, among them a rare edition of J.R.R. Tolkien's *Lord of the Rings*, and an immaculate first edition of *Harry Potter and the Chamber of Secrets*. *Chamber* was expected to raise over $1,000 in a charity auction.

Toward the end of the month, some controversy began to brew in England over the fact that a primary school teacher had forbidden students from reading the Harry Potter novels, claiming they went against the teachings of the Bible. Explained Carol Rookwood, "As a head teacher I have a responsibility to ensure that we give the children the best that we possibly can. We are a Church of

England–aided primary school, which means the church ethos is very important to what we do. The Bible is very clear and consistent in its teachings that wizards, devils and demons exist and are very real, powerful and dangerous, and God's people are told to have nothing to do with them." One place that Rookwood did *not* find support was with the National Secular Society, which responded, "Children's imaginations have been nourished for centuries with stories of wizards, witches and fairies. In this age of declining literacy, banning popular children's books is doing pupils a great disservice." Similar complaints arose in the United States, but J.K. Rowling insisted that she would not change her approach in dealing with the subjects of good and evil.

Warner Brothers announced that Chris Columbus, whose previous directorial efforts include the first two *Home Alone* films, *Bicentennial Man* and *Mrs. Doubtfire*, would be directing the adaptation of the first Harry novel. Columbus said at the time, "I'm thrilled and honored to bring the Harry Potter books to the screen. Between my four kids and all their friends, I've heard a lot about what this movie should be and how I could ruin if it I cut this or that scene. From the first time I read *Harry Potter* with my children, I fell in love with these wonderful characters and this world. I won't let anyone down. It will be a faithful adaptation."

On the choice of Columbus, producer David Heyman noted, "There was a lot of interest from numerous directors who wanted to be involved with Harry Potter, but Chris emerged as the person with the greatest passion and understanding of the books and the desire to remain faithful to Jo's vision." For his part, Columbus added, "I'd heard these horrendous and actually quite amusing stories about how certain directors had wanted to adapt the book, like changing the locale to a Hollywood high school or turning Harry Potter and Hermione into American students or making the entire film as a computer animated picture. I was stunned by some of these notions. I mean, it all feels painfully obvious to me. There's a reason why millions of children and adults have fallen in love with the Harry Potter books. To destroy the basic foundation of this world and these characters would alienate our audience. So I was adamant about being incredibly faithful to the books, which means shooting the films in England, with an all-British cast."

In another interview, Columbus relayed why doing the film was important to him. "Over the years," he explained, "people — particularly the media — have implied that I've gone soft because I've directed some sentimental films. But based on my own personal life at the time, I felt that those were films I needed to make. Once I got those stories out of my system, I wanted to go back to where I was when I started out as a writer, which is a much darker place. . . . I've always been a big fan of British cinema, everything from David Lean pictures, comedies like *Kind Hearts and Coronets*, emotional dramas like *A Man for All Seasons* and particularly the Hammer horror films, which I adored. I found them very atmospheric and evocative. I grew up watching these films, and they influenced my early writing." In particular he referred to the script he had written for *Young Sherlock Holmes*, which was "set at a British boarding school and involved two pre-teen boys and a girl who solve a supernatural mystery. It was sort of preparation for directing *Harry Potter*."

April 2000

According to the BBC, booksellers in England reported that the paperback edition of *Harry Potter and the Prisoner of Azkaban* were outselling all other children's books by a margin of about five to one. One bookstore owner proclaimed, "It's just been flying off the shelves, a lot of people have obviously been waiting for the book for a while."

June 2000

With the fourth book (whose title was still being kept under wraps) scheduled for publication on July 8, word began leaking out that bookstores in both America and in Britain were planning Harry Potter parties to celebrate its arrival, inviting kids to come in costume and enjoy a number of activities, including watching magicians. Reported the *San Francisco Chronicle*, "Many retailers are planning to stay open until 1 a.m. — a move that seems extreme, considering that Harry Potter's main audience is children. Some stores are even planning pajama parties — a Zany Brainy outlet in North Carolina, for instance, is inviting kids to spend the night. Harry Potter parties will be held in thousands of bookstores July 8, and even public libraries are planning special 'first chapter' readings of the new book — provided the librarians grab a copy quick before they fly out the door." Tracy Wynne, the co-owner of the San Francisco bookstore Cover to Cover, enthused, "If an author can get so many kids reading a 700-page book, it will be a miracle for literacy."

In the month prior to the fourth book's publication, the *Washington Post* made note of the fact that despite Scholastic publishing the books in the United States, they controlled none of the merchandising rights to Harry Potter. That particular honor

A coven of young Harry Potter fans waits outside a Waterstone's on London's Oxford Street for the release of the latest Harry Potter instalment. (Jane Mingay/AP Photo)

belonged to Warner Brothers, which acquired them along with the motion picture rights. "The licensing machine is already up and running," offered the paper, "even though the movie won't be released until November 16, 2001. Warner Brothers is already predicting Harry Potter merchandise will rival that of its Batman franchise, which has brought more than $1 billion to the company from the sale of everything from T-shirts to coffee mugs." At that point, the studio had already signed 46 licensing deals for Harry merchandise, with more anticipated. "To put the $1 billion that Warner Brothers expects to bring in from merchandise in perspective," said the *Post*, "Scholastic Press will ring up $100 million in U.S. sales from the first four novels."

Scotland's St. Andrews University bestowed upon J.K. Rowling an honorary degree, making her a Doctor of Letters. Director of External Relations Sue Cunningham said, "Jo Rowling has shown that children's books are still capable of capturing and enchanting an immense audience, irrespective of the competing attractions of television, Nintendo, Gameboy and Pokémon. At a time when dire predictions were being made for the future of books, children are rediscovering the pure joy of reading." Along the same lines, the *Washington Post* mused, "Is Rowling on a roll? Is she single-handedly leading a new generation to the extreme pleasures of total immersion in a book? Will today's Potter-lovers be toasting Tolstoy tomorrow? Marching through *Middlemarch*? Zealous for Zola? Delighting in Dante and Dickens and Dostoevsky? Or is she pushing her luck by writing such an epic adventure? Can she continue to overcome nanosecond attention spans and Dreamcast mentalities? Will she lose readers in her labyrinthine world, like so many people with a penchant for Thomas Pynchon who lapped up the 152-page *The Crying of Lot 49* but got hopelessly lost in the 784-page *Gravity's Rainbow?*"

Scandal erupted toward the end of the month, as Salon.com pointed out: "Despite a level of security that's been compared to that of the CIA, the British and American publishers of J.K. Rowling's bestselling series of Harry Potter novels were unable to keep the title of Book IV a secret until the book's on-sale date of July 8. The *London Telegraph* reported Sunday that 'sources close to the project' strongly hinted that the title of the new book is *Harry Potter and the Goblet of Fire*." Seeing no choice, Scholastic admitted that the report was true. "It was leaked," offered the publisher's Judy Corman, "and once that happened, we felt it was silly to try keeping it a secret. It was going to be a surprise, like a birthday or Christmas present, for the kids. We're sorry, but we know they'll like the book just the same." The same article made mention of the fact that Maggie Smith was up for the role of Professor McGonagall and Tim Roth as Professor Snape.

The BBC jumped on the story about the leaked book title simultaneously providing info on just how well the novel was doing prior to its publication. "The print run for *Harry Potter and the Goblet of Fire* has set a new publishing record with one million copies in the first run," they noted. "A representative for Amazon.co.uk said the book had also smashed all records for a book sold online, with hundreds of pre-orders flooding in daily. Extra staff have been recruited at the online bookseller's distribution center to cope with the anticipated demand, and security has been tightened to ensure nobody reveals the plot ahead of the book's official launch on 8 July. . . . Only a handful of executives have read the novel, and in the U.S., the publisher's manuscript is said to be under armed guard at a compound in Wisconsin."

The search for the perfect child to play Harry Potter began in earnest. Reporter Josh Grossberg noted, "Hopeful Harrys who fit the Brit, 9 to 11 profile were asked to send a picture and videotape of themselves stating their name and age, telling a joke and reading a paragraph from any of the three Potter novels. Producers are also looking for talented tykes to play Potter pals Hermione Granger and Ron Weasley — friends from the Hogwarts School of Witchcraft and Wizardry — as well as Harry's school nemesis, Draco Malfoy. During the first stage of auditions, casting agents filmed the children reading a page in the book. If called back a second time, they were filmed improvising a scene when the young wizards first arrive at Hogwarts. The third call back had the prospective Potter reading from three pages of the script with the director in attendance."

July 2000

Eight-year-old Laura Cantwell stunned pretty much everyone by getting her hands on a copy of *Harry Potter and the Goblet of Fire* about a week before its publication date. As reported in the press, a friend of the family came across eight copies of the novel on sale at a Northern Virginia bookstore. Reported *The Washington Post*, "The friend said she went to the counter — where the clerk didn't even blink — and walked out with two copies. It was the literary equivalent of walking out of the Smithsonian having just bought the Hope Diamond." To her credit, Laura never revealed any aspects of the novel to anyone, but did, in fact, find herself becoming something of a minor celebrity. She was interviewed by a number of newspapers and even made an appearance on NBC's *Today Show*.

BusinessWeek Online exposed a controversy of a different sort when it reported that independent booksellers were up in arms over the fact that Amazon.com was promising that the first 350,000 people to order the new novel would receive it on the day of publication, just hours after the official release. "Members of the American Booksellers Association are upset because in making arrangements to have the new Potter book shipped to their stores, they had to sign detailed affidavits with publisher Scholastic Inc. pledging to not even open boxes of the book until midnight of July 8. The indies accuse Scholastic of cutting a special deal with Amazon. They say it's just another example of how release rules don't apply to the book-world giants, such as Amazon.com. If not, how could Amazon possibly overnight so many books to its customers on July 7 without opening the boxes or ensuring the Federal Express delivery person didn't get a peek at the Potter cover? Michael Jacobs, senior vice-president of trade at Scholastic Inc., the U.S. arm of the global publisher, maintains that no covert deal was made."

As *The Goblet of Fire* was preparing to fly off bookshelves, it was becoming obvious that adults were enjoying Harry Potter's adventures as much as children were. Noted the *Washington Post*, "Turns out, adult fans of the J.K. Rowling books have read (and sometimes re-read) all three of the earlier books and ordered an advance copy of the fourth, due for release tonight. . . . Market researchers have yet to calculate the number of adult readers, but they do know that grown-ups have done their part to boost demand for Harry Potter. Estimates are that 43 percent of the books sold in 1999 were bought for people older than 14. . . . Bookstore owners from Gaithersburg to Capital Hill say that adult fans are freely declaring they aren't just parents buying another Potter book for their children. And some adults are recommending Potter books to co-workers and friends." Actually, the adult appeal of the novels was not lost on the publishers, when, beginning with the publication of *Harry Potter and the Prisoner of Azkaban*, two sets of covers were offered for the novels, one designed for children, the other darker and definitely designed for an adult readership.

In response to the demand for *Goblet of Fire*, the BBC offered this comment from J.K. Rowling: "I wrote the book for me, this is all a bit of a shock and I'm amazed — think of a stronger word and double it."

Salon.com said of the whole *Goblet of Fire* phenomenon, "On an unseasonally cool night for July in Manhattan, people began lining up in front of the Upper West Side Barnes & Noble bookstore at about 10 p.m. Friday. By the time the feverishly awaited book went on sale at midnight, the line had stretched to include almost 350 people. Like most of the bookstores that stayed open late to sell the book, this one had thrown itself into the event. The staff were dressed in witch and wizard costumes and the store was decorated with bunches of star-shaped balloons, plastic spiders and a few cauldrons besides enormous, ziggurat-like piles of the previous three books in J.K. Rowlings' popular series." Very appropriately, writer Laura Miller concluded with, "As I rode home on the subway surrounded by people who sat happily with open copies of *Goblet* on their laps, what struck me as most extraordinary about the event was neither the lines nor the TV cameras nor the spectacle of kids going wild over a book. It was the knowledge, unprecedented in a life devoted to the solitary practice of reading, that last night and throughout this weekend, I and millions of other people, young and old, will all be reading the very same book."

BusinessWeek Online reported that the success of the Harry Potter books had tripled the stock worth of British publisher Bloomsbury Publishing. "The uproar," it was pointed out, "has created something unusual in the clubby world of British publishing: a bestseller circus that the Brits previously thought only vulgar Americans capable of perpetrating. . . ."

To help promote *The Goblet of Fire*, J.K. Rowling took to the rails. Reported the *Washington Post*, "With two ferocious shrieks of its whistle, a scarlet steam engine pulled away from Platform 9¾ at King's Cross Station this morning, carrying the world's most popular living author, J.K. Rowling, on a journey patterned on the magical train trips she created in her Harry Potter books. Rowling will ride the train, dubbed the Hogwarts Express, for the next four days on a promotional tour." The reason? Her gratitude to Bloomsbury Publishing for having picked up Harry Potter in the first place. The promotional tour, it should be pointed out, was more for children at each stop, members of which included contest winners who had won the right to meet with her in person.

The Hogwarts Express terminates at Hogsmeade Station, which is played by Goathland Station in North Yorkshire, England. (Fionna Boyle)

Amusingly, as reporters and photographers attempted to get close to Rowling, they were rejected with the statement that it was a "private function."

The *Indian Express* referred to the furor around the fourth Harry adventure as a "literary gold rush. No event in publishing history comes anywhere near matching the frenzy that has erupted over the last week in the run-up to the release of the book."

Surprisingly, the *Washington Post* expressed considerable skepticism regarding the movie version of *Harry Potter and the Sorcerer's Stone*, scheduled to begin shooting later in the year. "The prognosis is not good. 'The people who love Harry Potter have created a Harry

Potter universe in their heads,' explains David Thomson, author of *A Biographical Dictionary of Film*. The hazard, of course, is that people will over-expect. 'The more intensively that imaginative process has been undertaken, the more disappointing the film will be'." They also put down the choice of Chris Columbus as director and Steve Kloves as writer, and mentioned that those directors who had been in the running were Steven Spielberg, Brad Silberling, Jonathan Demme, Tim Robbins and Mike Newell (who eventually went on to shoot the adaptation of *Goblet of Fire*).

CNN.com offered an interview with stage actor Jim Dale regarding the fact that he had played 125 characters in the audiobook version of *Goblet of Fire*, following his reading of the first three novels. Of the experience he offered, "Whether I want to or not, I think I will be remembered for Harry Potter. How lovely to be remembered as the voice of Harry Potter. And to be perfectly honest, when you listen to the tapes, when you get to Harry, it's just a younger-sounding voice that you're hearing. I haven't tried to make him different from the voice I have. So it's nice to think my younger voice of myself is the voice that kids are hearing as Harry Potter." He also reflected on getting the gig in the first place: "Never having heard of Harry Potter, I said I'd like to read it. Having read it, I was immersed completely in the Harry Potter world. I recognized that this was something exceptionally clever and very good and very well written, with a prospect of six more books to follow. So of course, this really whetted my appetite and I immediately said, 'Yes.'"

A rumor making the rounds was that an American named Liam Aiken — who had worked with Chris Columbus on *Stepmom* — was going to be cast as Harry. When asked about it, Rowling responded, "Ignore the Internet, ignore the *Daily Express*. Harry has not been cast yet. And believe me, he's going to be British when he is." Most people, of course, didn't realize that that was actually part of the deal negotiated with Warner Brothers.

August 2000

The rumor mill began heating up regarding who would play Harry in the upcoming film, with 13-year-old British actor Gabriel Thomson rumored to be in the running (which Thomson and his agent both denied). Oscar winner Haley Joel Osment expressed interest in the role, though obviously he didn't get it.

In an interview with *Entertainment Weekly*, J.K. Rowling discussed the themes of bigotry that are explored in *Goblet of Fire*. "Bigotry is probably the thing I detest most," she said. "All forms of intolerance, the whole idea of 'that which is different from me is necessarily evil.' I really like to explore the idea that difference is equal and good. But there's another idea that I like to explore, too. Oppressed groups are not, generally speaking, people who stand firmly together. No, sadly, they kind of subdivide among themselves and fight like hell. That's human nature, so that's what you see here. This world of wizards and witches, they're already ostracized, and then within themselves they've formed a loathsome pecking order." In the same interview she was asked what the experience in Hollywood had been like. "The person I was most nervous about meeting by far was Steve Kloves," she admitted, "who's writing the screenplay. I was really ready to hate [him]. This was the man who was gonna butcher my baby. The first time I met him, he said, 'You know who my favorite character is?' And I thought, 'You're gonna say Ron.' It's real easy to love Ron, but so obvious. But he said, 'Hermione.' I just kind of melted."

A deal was struck for the 900-year-old Gloucester Cathedral to

Director Chris Columbus poses with Daniel Radcliffe, days after the boy had been chosen from thousands of applicants to play Harry Potter in the films. (Dave Caulkin/AP Photo)

double as Hogwarts in the first Harry film. The Reverend Nicholas Bury mused, "It is one of the most beautiful cathedrals and its friendliness and human scale have often been remarked upon. It is a good place for a story about a young boy making friends in his first year at an unusual school."

A school head in Singapore proclaimed that children should not read the Harry Potter novels as they could be an "anti-Christian influence."

On August 21, Warner Brothers announced that 11-year-old Daniel Radcliffe had been signed for the lead role, and that he would be joined by Emma Watson as Hermione and Rupert Grint as Ron. Said the studio's Lorenzo di Bonaventura, "We searched through all the Muggle and Wizard households just to find the right young people to play Harry, Ron and Hermione and we have found them in Dan, Rupert and Emma. These are magical roles, the kind that come around once in a lifetime, and they required talented children who can bring magic to the screen." Chris Columbus added, "We had seen so many enormously talented kids in the search for Harry. The process was intense and there were times when we felt we would never find an individual who embodied the complex spirit and depth of Harry Potter. Then Dan walked into the room and we all knew we had found Harry. We were equally elated upon meeting Emma and Rupert. I couldn't be happier to work with such talented, young actors." In response to the casting news, J.K. Rowling enthused, "Having seen Dan Radcliffe's screen test, I don't think Chris Columbus could have found a better Harry. I wish Dan, Emma and Rupert the very best of luck, and hope they have as much fun acting the first year at Hogwarts as I had writing it."

David Heyman elaborated on the casting process, explaining, "It was not easy to find a boy who embodied the many qualities of Harry Potter. We wanted someone who could combine a sense of wonder and curiosity, the sense of having lived a life, having experienced pain; an old soul in a child's body. He needed to be open and generous to those around him and have good judgment. Harry is not great at academics; he has flaws. But that's what makes him so compelling, so human — that he's not perfect. Harry has an 'everyman' quality, yet he is capable of great things. He makes us all believe that magic is possible."

Chris Columbus provided more detail on the casting process of the Harry character: "We had auditioned hundreds of potential Harry Potters, and I was still unhappy with the results. The first casting director, in a fit of total frustration, threw up her arms and said, 'I just don't know what you want!' Sitting on a shelf in the office was a video copy of *David Copperfield*, starring Daniel Radcliffe. I picked up the video box, pointed to Dan's face and said, 'This is who I want! This is Harry Potter.' The casting director said, 'I've told you before, he is unavailable and his parents aren't interested in him doing this film.'" Added Heyman, "I completely understood their reticence and caution in allowing their child to play a role that would inevitably change his life. But we arranged a meeting over tea that afternoon with Dan. We talked for an hour and a half. His energy and enthusiasm were wonderful. I had a feeling that this was our Harry." Noted Columbus, "To the Radcliffes' credit, they were totally aware of the enormity of the project and for the sake of their child, were not going to make this decision lightly. We made it very clear to them that we would protect their son. We knew from the start that Dan was Harry Potter. He has the magic, the inner depth and darkness that is very rare in an 11-year-old. He also has a sense of wisdom and intelligence that I haven't seen in many other kids his age. We knew we had made the right choice after sending Jo a copy of Daniel's screen test. Jo's comment was something to the effect of, 'It's as if I've been reunited with my long-lost son.'"

In an interview, Daniel Radcliffe reflected on getting the role of Harry: "I thought there are millions of boys auditioning for that part, and I know I won't get it. But I was in the bath and talking to my mom when the phone rang and dad came in and told me I'd got the part. I was so happy, I cried a lot! That night I woke up at two in the morning and woke up mom and dad and I asked them, 'Is it real? Am I dreaming?' I was so excited."

On the casting of Rupert Grint and Emma Watson, Columbus pointed out, "We'd been simultaneously looking to fill the other roles, but the casting of Harry was the peak of the triangle, and without him, none of the rest would make sense. We brought in several children for screen tests, but it soon became apparent who were the three. We immediately fell in love with Rupert Grint. He's extremely funny and has such an incredibly warm presence. Emma Watson embodies the soul and the essence of Hermione Granger. When we saw Dan, Rupert and Emma together on

Rupert Grint, Daniel Radcliffe, and Emma Watson pose with director Chris Columbus, Richard Harris (Dumbledore), Robbie Coltrane (Hagrid), and producer David Heyman. (Adam Butler/AP Photo)

screen, they had amazing chemistry. It was electric. We knew we had found the perfect team."

Rupert Grint offered, "Ron is one of my favorite characters and I can really relate to him. I've got loads of brothers and sisters, and I know what it's like growing up in a big family. And I still get hand-me-downs. . . . I was watching *Newsround* and they told us how you could audition for a part in the Harry Potter film. I sent in a form and a photograph and a month went by and I heard nothing. Then I was on the *Newsround* Web site and found out that one boy sent in a video of himself reading a little piece from the script. So I put together a video, sent it over and I got an audition."

"When I read the book," Emma Watson noted to the press, "I thought that Hermione would be a great character to play. But I had to go through a lot of auditions. It wasn't easy. Then one day, they sat Rupert and I down in David Heyman's office and simply told us we'd got the part. It didn't sink in at first. I just stood there looking blankly at them for about two minutes. . . . Unlike Hermione, I've never been top of my class. In fact, quite the opposite. Although I am very bossy and my little brother tends to suffer a bit."

The following day, the *Guardian Unlimited* noted that also cast in the film were Maggie Smith, Robbie Coltrane and Alan Rickman. Additionally, the BBC ran a story in which Radcliffe was quoted as saying, "A lot of the other boys in my class know I've read the first one or two books, and they've read all of them and they're a bit angry because I have read the least Harry Potter books." He also added, "I went on the broomstick yesterday and flew around a big room, and that was really fun. I think I'm a tiny bit like Harry, because I'd like to have an owl." Added Emma Watson, "Normally, every night my daddy reads two chapters. At the moment, we're on the fourth book but we haven't yet completed it." For Rupert's part, he noted, "I think I'm scarily like my character. I live in a family of seven and have a redheaded sister." Chris Columbus explained that his experience with Macaulay Culkin on the *Home Alone* films taught him a great lesson on how to work with young actors. "When I got involved with the first *Home Alone*, I didn't know what I was letting myself in for with child actors," he admitted. "I learned a big lesson and I was concerned that when we dealt with the children, we should make certain the parents were wonderful, because I felt the need to protect these kids against the onslaught of publicity."

The *Register* reported that German fans who had grown impatient with the time lag between the publication of *Goblet of Fire* in English and in their native tongue had decided to translate chapters and post them on the Internet. German publisher Carlsen Verlag immediately got a court injunction filed against them. The translated chapter quickly came offline.

September 2000

China was ready to receive more than half a million copies of *The Goblet of Fire* — the largest first-edition run of a work of fiction in that country in over 50 years — but had to push the date forward because of bootleg translated editions.

In an interview with the BBC, J.K. Rowling said that some of the material in her books might not be suitable for younger children. "I do think that, on occasion, the material is not suitable for six-year-olds," she said. "But you can't stop them reading it. I read things when I was very young that disturbed me, but I don't think that was a terribly bad thing. My parents never censored what I read, so I wouldn't say don't read them to a six-year-old, just be aware some of it does get uncomfortable. I am dealing with evil — I am trying to examine what happens to this community when a maniac tries to take over. If you are going to write about those kinds of things, you have a moral obligation to show what that involves, not to prettify it or to minimize it."

October 2000

Given her background, it should hardly be surprising that Rowling accepted the post of ambassador for the National Council for One

Parent Families (NCOPF). To commemorate the occasion, she delivered a speech in which she said, "It is definitely time we exploded the popular myth that most of us are feckless teenagers trying to get council flats. Six out of 10 families headed by a single parent are living in poverty. But none of the lone parents I know want to live on handouts; just like parents living in couples, we want the chance to provide properly for our own children. Single parenthood is not all stress and hardship. My flesh-and-blood daughter is the best thing that ever happened to me, including my fictional son. I had a degree, a profession and friends who were willing and able to lend me money when I badly needed it. So if I met obstacles in pulling myself out of the benefit system and back into employment, how much more difficult must it be for people who don't have the same advantages? If I experienced the feeling of utter, utter worthlessness with the CSA (Child Support Agency) and the benefit office, how many other parents are going through the same right now?" Besides the speech, Rowling reportedly donated £500,000 to the NCOPF.

On October 20, 10 Harry Potter essay winners were escorted by J.K. Rowling to NBC's *Today* show and then to Harry's American publisher, Scholastic, before they were given a number of Harry gifts. The subject of their essays was "How the Harry Potter Books Have Changed My Life." Said Rowling, "They write well. It's not just what they said, but how they said it."

The BBC reported that due to a character mix-up in a scene, Bloomsbury was forced to reprint millions of copies of *Goblet of Fire* with the mistake corrected. In the first edition, Fudge, the minister of magic, is confused with Crouch, a villain who was featured earlier in the book but was not mentioned after that.

On the 21st, J.K. Rowling revealed a few interesting Harry tidbits to the *Sunday Oregonian*, not the least of which was the fact that the two small books she had written — *Fantastic Beasts and Where to Find Them* and *Quidditch through the Ages* — were written to benefit the Comic Relief charity.

John Cleese was announced in the role of Nearly Headless Nick, the ghost of Gryffindor Tower, and actress Julie Walters was cast as Ron's mother, Mrs. Weasley.

J.K. Rowling appeared at Toronto's Skydome Stadium to address 10,000 gathered Harry Potter fans. She read them chapter four of *Goblet of Fire* and took questions. At one point she admitted, "I am delighted and terrified to be here."

Controversy broke out in America and abroad over the notion that the Harry Potter novels were promoting Satanism, a claim that Rowling herself debunked by replying to one accuser, "No, but you are a lunatic." It should be pointed out that from almost the beginning Harry has found himself banned from certain libraries and has been the subject of book burnings.

While in New York, Rowling made two appearances on NBC's *Today* show. Interestingly, in 2006 people have been conjecturing whether or not Harry will die in book seven. But when Katie Couric asked her about the possibility of novels that follow an adult Harry, Rowling replied, "I'm intrigued because everyone seems very confident I'm not going to kill him. I'm not saying either way. Everyone assumes that there will be an adult life, and maybe they're right."

Also on *Today*, Rowling revealed that the name of the next novel, book five, would be *Harry Potter and the Order of the Phoenix*. "I kept saying I wouldn't tell anyone," she laughed, "but this cute boy, about eight, asked me and I knew it would make him so happy."

November 2000

When *Harry Potter and the Philosopher's Stone* was published in 1997, there were only 500 copies printed, 200 in paperback and 300 in hardcover. In auction, one of those books sold for nearly $10,000.

Although nine-year-old Natalie McDonald's attempts to reach J.K. Rowling before her death from leukemia weren't successful, the author, not knowing the little girl had died, wrote back, touching Natalie's parents with the obvious care put into the response. A friendship was struck up between Rowling and Natalie's family, and as *Maclean's* detailed it, "On page 159 of *Goblet of Fire*, the famous sorting hat of Hogwarts School of Witchcraft and Wizardry sends first-year student Natalie McDonald — the only real person named in any of Rowling's novels — to Harry's own Gryffindor house."

The BBC reported that J.K. Rowling was named Scotland's top earner for the year, having pulled in nearly $50 million from Harry Potter.

BBC Radio 4 announced that they would be broadcasting comic actor Stephen Fry reading the entire text of *Philosopher's Stone* to listeners. A BBC spokesperson noted, "When I became controller I was determined, if I could, to get Harry Potter on Radio 4. I would like there to be a generation of children in their 20s who will look back and remember listening to the radio on Boxing Day, because Harry Potter is part of their imaginative landscape. I'd be amazed if people listened intently for eight hours. I think there will be people who

The Hogwarts Dining Hall was modeled after the dining hall at Christ Church College, at Oxford University. (Fionna Boyle)

keep it on all day and dip in, mentally, in and out." Added Fry, "Reading Harry Potter books out loud is more fun than I feel a single human being could ever deserve. It's like swimming in chocolate."

Hail to the Wizard? The Department of Education held a "Vote to Read" campaign in which children could vote for whoever they wanted to be president and vice president, as long as those people came from works of fiction. Harry Potter got the bid for pres, while Clifford the Big Red Dog was the choice for VP.

Despite the fact that by this point the Harry Potter novels had sold over 43 million copies, Rowling insisted that her drive to continue his adventures had not waned. "I have been writing about Harry for 10 years," said the author. "He's very real to me. I think I'm quite driven on this. I want to get this story out of me. It's that simple. There's no other reason to keep writing."

Warner Brothers sent a cease and desist letter to 15-year-old Claire Field, claiming that she had no right to have the Internet domain name harrypotterguide.co.uk. There would ultimately be considerable back-and-forth on this, but in the end the ridiculousness of the claim became apparent and Claire was allowed to keep her fan site.

December 2000

As evidence that Harry Potter had become big business, Warner Brothers won the legal case it raised against a company named HarperStephens, based in California, which had been accused of cyber-squatting by registering 107 Potter-related web domain names in an effort to be paid serious money for the rights to those domains. It was ruled that HarperStephens had "no rights or legitimate interests" in them and therefore had registered in bad faith.

To help raise money for a cancer charity, J.K. Rowling offered a book reading in Glasgow, Scotland.

Harry continued his phenomenal success around the world, becoming a big hit in Vietnam, among many other places.

An 11-year-old Oregon girl named Annie Rose Favreau won a contest in which participants had to write a letter to Harry Potter. Betsy Howie of Scholastic Book Clubs, which sponsored the contest, responded to Annie, "The exceptional creativity, clarity and use of language in your entry really made it stand out from the rest. That speaks very highly of your work since many of the letters reviewed by our judges were truly superb." As a reward, Annie received a trunk filled with Harry Potter merchandise, including a signed copy of the first novel.

The United Nations' World Intellectual Property Organization decreed that Warner Brothers' parent company, Time Warner, holds exclusive rights to domain names including Harry Potter, thus squashing the efforts of so-called cyber-squatters.

January 2001

When drug paraphernalia (though no drugs) was found on the British sets for the first Harry Potter film, production was called to a halt and everyone sent home until the situation was cleared up. Noted a studio spokesperson, "As we address this very serious matter, our paramount concern is for the safety and protection of the cast and crew of *Harry Potter*. Warner Brothers Pictures will continue to work closely with the production to ensure the highest level of security is enforced on the set and at the production facility."

A 30-second clip of *Harry Potter and the Sorcerer's Stone* was aired during Super Bowl XXXV.

February 2001

In an interview with the Ain't It Cool News Web site, Harry Potter screenwriter Steve Kloves mused, "Hopefully people will love the world and stuff, because we didn't monkey with it. We didn't say, 'Okay, now we gotta add something here in the beginning.' We're just going to trust that the audience will hang with it. It's faithful."

According to British news reports, production nearly shut down on *Harry Potter* due to a legal question of how much time Daniel

Radcliffe was working each day and whether or not his on-set education was being handled properly. "Although Daniel attends a private school," noted a government spokesperson, "his application for permission to work must come to us and we must be satisfied that his education is being organized properly. It is our statutory duty to consider this and to worry about exploitation." Any difficulties were ironed out.

Warner Brothers signed with Coca-Cola for the soda company to be Harry's sole promotional partner, a deal worth about $150 million.

Due to delays based on weather, Warners had to get legal permission for Daniel Radcliffe's shooting schedule to be extended from the end of March to mid-July. In the end, of course, the request was granted.

March 2001

For all she had done for children's literature, J.K. Rowling was given Britain's highest honor, the OBE (Order of the British Empire).

During an interview with Raincoast Books, the Canadian publisher of the Harry Potter books, Rowling discussed the genesis of the books *Quidditch through the Ages* and *Fantastic Beasts and Where to Find Them*. "I got a letter from Richard Curtis who started Comic Relief saying, 'Would you consider writing us a short story?' And then he cunningly said something like, 'I'm sure you won't, we'll still love your books, even if you don't, but just thought we'd ask.' Which is a very clever way of asking someone to do some-

thing. But I didn't need much persuasion as I have always sup-
ported Comic Relief, and I think they do fantastic work. So I
wrote back and said yes, but I'm not good at short stories — particularly short Harry stories. I tend to ramble on, so how would it
be if I wrote a couple of the titles that appear as titles in the
novels? So that's how it all started. And I decided to do two, just
because I had two in my head and I couldn't really decide between
Fantastic Beasts and *Quidditch*."

Pennsylvania author Nancy Stouffer did end up launching a lawsuit against J.K. Rowling and her publishers, claiming that many
elements of Harry's world were taken from her book, *The Legend of
Rah and the Muggles*. Said Stouffer, "I have been accused of stealing;
some children believe I am the one that followed J.K. Rowling."
According to the BBC, "In Stouffer's *Rah and the Muggles*, which features a character named Larry Potter, the muggles are little people
who care for two orphaned boys who magically turn their dark
homeland into a happy place." Eventually Scholastic and Warner
Brothers launched a countersuit against Stouffer.

The first movie trailer for *Harry Potter and the Sorcerer's Stone*
appeared in theaters, giving fans one minute and 47 seconds of
Potter live-action magic.

Queen Elizabeth spent a day exploring different aspects of the
British book industry. Among her stops was Harry Potter publisher
Bloomsbury, where she met with, among others, J.K. Rowling. The
Queen noted of her son, Prince Charles, "He knows the books well
and likes them. I would like to think other members of the royal
family would also like them."

Fiona Shaw, who plays Harry's Aunt Petunia in the films, reflected
on *Sorcerer's Stone* to the BBC, saying, "I had a ball doing *Harry
Potter*, and Christopher Columbus' values seem to be bang on,

Queen Elizabeth meets with J.K. Rowling during a day-long tour of the British book industry. (Stefan Rousseau/Reuters/Corbis)

with the attention to emotional detail very much in place. That is what will make the film, not the hype or the special effects."

April 2001

Stephen Fry's 21-hour reading of *Harry Potter and the Goblet of Fire* generated tremendous amounts of advance sales for the CD set. J.K. Rowling insisted on the length, noting, "I just said, 'Let's do the whole thing or not at all. I've yet to meet a kid who was sorry we did it that way." Added Helen Nicoll of Cover to Cover, "Many children and adults like to have the books in audio format as well as in print, because you get a different type of enjoyment for each."

Rowling, Warner Brothers and Electronic Arts announced that a deal had been struck to develop a new Harry Potter online game.

Intervisual Books, Inc. struck a deal with Scholastic to create a pair of "interactive" Harry Potter titles. Said Intervisual's Norm Sheinman, "We are delighted to have this opportunity to produce these exciting Harry Potter books for Scholastic. . . . The first book will be in the classic pop-up format with 3D action scenes bringing to life the magical adventures of Harry Potter. The second is a book/playset version of the mysterious, three-dimensional castle known as Hogwarts School of Wizardry."

A report stated that J.K. Rowling's personal wealth had swelled to nearly $100 million.

The young Harry Potter cast was required to sign nondisclosure agreements by Warner Brothers This was explained by a spokeswoman, "As a matter of routine, we asked the parents or legal guardians of the children who are working on the set to sign these agreements. The purpose of them is to stop people discussing various aspects of the film before it's released."

May 2001

It was announced that the Harry Potter novels had sold over 100 million copies.

Lego debuted their line of Harry Potter products.

Rumors that J.K. Rowling was to marry Dr. Neil Murray, whom she had quietly begun dating, were debunked by her camp.

Although summer was just about to begin, the box office competition was already beginning to heat up as both *Harry Potter and the Sorcerer's Stone* and *Lord of the Rings: Fellowship of the Ring* were scheduled to compete during the same holiday season.

Composer John Williams met with director Chris Columbus to discuss the scoring of *Sorcerer's Stone*. Said Wiliams, "I imagine there will be a lot of music in the film, and Chris Columbus has told me that the film is long and that he needs to whittle it down. That's a very hard and heartbreaking process for a director, and it's very difficult for a composer, too."

When J.K. Rowling won the $1,418 prize from the Scottish Arts Council for *Goblet of Fire*, she immediately turned it over to the New Writer's Bursary Scheme, a fund designed to benefit new authors.

June 2001

Warner Brothers confirmed that the second *Sorcerer's Stone* trailer would be attached to prints of Steven Spielberg's *A.I.* for play in movie theaters.

Director Chris Columbus gave an interview to *USA Today* in which he expressed his desire to stay faithful to Rowling's novel. "To make this film, you have to be a fan," he said. "These books are incredibly imaginative, classic stories. Why would you need to toy with that? It was a passion for me to be as faithful as possible."

Rumors that Hugh Grant would be cast in the second film, *Harry Potter and the Chamber of Secrets*, turned out to be false.

Sotheby's announced that on the 10th they would be auctioning off original illustrations from the first Harry Potter novel.

July 2001

Rumors arose that Warner Brothers wanted $70 million for the TV rights to *Sorcerer's Stone*. The previous record holder had been the $30 million NBC paid for the rights to James Cameron's *Titanic*.

Fans seemed concerned that Harry's lightning-shaped scar on Daniel Radcliffe's forehead was not in the right place as described in the novels. The filmmakers told *Entertainment Weekly* that their instructions from J.K. Rowling were to make the scar be "razor sharp and just off center."

Game producers Wizards of the Coast struck a deal to create trading cards based on Harry Potter. The company's Elaine Chase pointed out, "There's a big appeal there. Every kid wants to turn out to be more than they think they are, and Harry gets to live that. Kids connect with him."

At the annual San Diego Comic Con, Warner Brothers unveiled a promotional sneak peek at *Sorcerer's Stone* that featured a number of sequences, all designed to whet the fans' appetites for the film before its November release.

August 2001

The British Tourist Authority announced plans to publish a Harry Potter map of Britain that would focus on key locations from the novels and new film.

Due to a longer-than-usual delay between books, rumors surfaced that J.K. Rowling was suffering from writer's block, resulting in a delay in the publication of *Harry Potter and the Order of the Phoenix*. First started in the newspaper *The Scotsman*, these rumors elicited a response from Rowling via letter. "As I, my publishers and my agent have stated since the publication of *Goblet of Fire* in July 2000, there was never any intention of publishing the fifth Harry Potter book in 2001. Nor has any deadline ever been set for the delivery of the manuscript. I made it clear last summer that I wanted to take the time to make sure that book five was not dashed off to meet a deadline. There is no writer's block — on the contrary, I am writing away very happily."

Rowling, who has always protected the privacy of her family, offered a formal protest against *OK!* magazine for printing photos of her eight-year-old daughter in a bikini.

Harry's creator took home the Walpole Medal of Excellence in her hometown of Edinburgh. Committee chairman Rupert Hambro noted, "We think she embodies everything to do with British excellence. She is the best-known author in the country, she is just about to launch a film, she is in the middle of writing her fifth book. She is an excellent product to advertise the country."

Alnwick Castle in Northumberland was used for the exteriors of Hogwarts in the first two Harry Potter films. The castle has set up cardboard cut-outs of the characters throughout the grounds. (Fionna Boyle)

According to *The Daily Record*, production on the first Harry film was delayed and the train standing in for the Hogwarts Express remained unmoving while the train station needed for the scene was widened.

September 2001

In an interview with the *New York Post*, Steven Spielberg admitted for the first time his real reasons for dropping out of the directorial running of *Harry Potter and the Sorcerer's Stone*. "I purposely didn't do the Harry Potter movie because, for me, that was shooting ducks in a barrel. It's just a slam dunk. It's just like withdrawing a billion dollars and putting it into your personal bank accounts. There's no challenge." In the pages of *The Telegraph* he added, "The first story didn't touch me creatively. Now the third Harry Potter book. . . . it's pure genius. Much darker, more esoteric and interesting to me personally. If they'd offered me that, I'd have said yes."

In an interview with *Vanity Fair* magazine, J.K. Rowling was extremely enthusiastic regarding the upcoming first film based on her work. "I've been watching it in my head for nine years now," she explained, "and finally I'll get to see it along with everybody else. The vital thing for me was that it would be true to the book, and I have great faith in Warner's commitment to that."

It was announced that the world premiere for *Sorcerer's Stone* would be on November 4 in London at the Odeon Cinema located in Leicester Square.

While speaking to *Nickelodeon Magazine*, Harry star Daniel Radcliffe admitted, "The first day on the set, I was very nervous. I was used to rehearsing with about eight other people, and then I got to the set and — including the extras — there were, like, 150 people there." He also pointed out that he did many of his own stunts: "There was one shot where I was hanging one hundred feet

The grounds of Alnwick Castle were where the first-year Gryffindors learned to fly in Harry Potter and the Sorcerer's Stone. *(Fionna Boyle)*

[away] from my broomstick, 22 feet in the air. I was wired up to the broom, with a huge airbag underneath me, and they moved me around up there. That was pretty cool."

J.K. Rowling was among those honored at the Whitaker Gold and Platinum Book Awards because her novels had been such an enormous presence on the bestseller lists over the previous four years.

Britain's toy store chain The Entertainer announced that they would not be carrying Harry Potter merchandise for fear it would attract children to the world of the occult. As silly as it may seem, this was just the latest in a wide-ranging, and long-running, controversy both in America and abroad concerning whether or not there was a darker subtext to the Harry Potter novels that celebrated evil over good. In the end, of course, the *vast* majority of people believed the opposite to be true.

October 2001

British undergraduate student Michele Fry saw her thesis —
*Heroes and Heroines: Myth and Gender Roles in the Harry Potter
Books* — published in an academic journal. Noted Fry, "Most
critics argue Hermione is an accessory, but I would say she is the
real power behind Harry Potter. Without her, he could not beat
the evil villain Voldemort."

Corporate tie-ins for *Harry Potter and the Sorcerer's Stone* had to be
handled gingerly, as J.K. Rowling did not want her creation to be
overly exploited. As a result, Coca-Cola's $150 million deal allowed
them to put Harry Potter "imagery" on its products *without* utilizing
photos of the film's cast. One part of the promotional program was
for Coca-Cola to donate $18 million to the Reading Is Fundamental
program in the United States, which encourages literacy in children. Coca-Cola consultant Manny Goldman pointed out that
"Harry Potter is the right direction to take. Coca-Cola is supposed
to be about something special and this is something special."

George Lucas's Industrial Light and Magic was awarded the effects
job for *Harry Potter and the Chamber of Secrets*.

Returning director Chris Columbus told the media that filming
had already begun on the second film, even though the first hadn't
even reached theaters yet.

Among the merchandise manufacturers tying into the first film
were Lego, Mattel, Tiger Electronics and Electronic Arts.

In a bid to raise money for the MS Society of Scotland, the QXL Web site auctioned off a dozen tickets to the preview screening of *Harry Potter and the Sorcerer's Stone*.

Actor Kenneth Branagh was announced to play Professor Gilderoy Lockhart in *Harry Potter and the Chamber of Secrets*. Offered Chris Columbus, "Ken is one of the great stage and screen actors of our time, and a great filmmaker. He's a perfect fit for our all-British ensemble, and he's one of the few younger actors who can hold his own against the likes of Richard Harris, Maggie Smith and Alan Rickman. I couldn't conceive of anyone else playing Gilderoy Lockhart." David Heyman elaborated, "Lockhart is amongst the most challenging roles in either of the two films. We needed someone who could be both annoying and charming, who would embrace Lockhart's narcissism, be hysterically funny, and still keep him grounded in reality."

Kenneth Branagh shared his feelings about being cast in the film: "It was nerve-wracking, because I was aware that *Chamber of Secrets* is a major film with huge audience expectations and that fans already had a very established idea of who Lockhart is. He's very flamboyant, rather vain and terribly narcissistic. So he's a delicious character to play, ferociously irritating and charming, but we had to convince audiences that he could have done all the things he claims. We had to make him plausible. I trusted Chris Columbus and his comic timing implicitly."

Detroit's Star Theatres announced that they would have a gala premiere on November 16, the proceeds of which would go to benefit the Food Bank of Oakland County and Gleaners Community Food Bank.

Bertie Bott's Every Flavor Beans offered up 38 flavors of jelly beans tied in to *Harry Potter and the Sorcerer's Stone*, among them sardine, horseradish and booger. The company's VP Deirdre Gonzalez stated, "There was some serious consideration given to the bodily fluid flavors. We thought, at the end of the day, do we really want to do that? [But] the people who read [the books] want to live in Harry's world. They want to be Harry Potter. Bertie Bott's are the only artificial product on the market. They're exactly what Harry Potter would be tasting if he were a real person."

Some skeptics voiced concern about *Sorcerer*'s running time of 152 minutes, but Dan Jolin of *Total Film* magazine philosophically offered, "A hundred million people in the world have read these books and loved them, and there's a sense of the longer, the better, even for children."

Reuters reported that props stolen from the set of the Harry Potter films were beginning to show up on eBay.

According to *USA Today*, advance ticket sales for the first Harry film were phenomenal. The newspaper quoted www.fandango.com's John Singh as saying, "There is Harry Potter mania everywhere. It's 15 days before the movie opens, and we're seeing the kind of volume we would normally see *one* day before a blockbuster opens."

November 2001

In an article appearing in *USA Today*, it was revealed that *Harry Potter and the Sorcerer's Stone* was produced at a cost of $125 million, its running time would be two hours and thirty-three min-

Emma Watson, Daniel Radcliffe and Rupert Grint at the premiere of Harry Potter and the Sorcerer's Stone. *(Gregory Pace/Corbis)*

utes, the film would be dubbed in 24 languages and subtitled in 16 more, it would open on over 4,000 screens in the United States and Canada, and almost simultaneously in 130 different countries.

Rumors that Daniel Radcliffe's voice broke during filming, thus requiring dubbing from a soundalike, were denied by Warner Brothers.

The London premiere of *Harry Potter and the Sorcerer's Stone* was a *major* success, with thousands of fans turning out alongside the red carpet at London's Leicester Square. Numerous stars from film and music attended the event.

Some interesting "rules" governing the Harry Potter films came to light. According to the *Los Angeles Times*, "The Harry Potter rules dictated that all partners had to know the books and follow them faithfully, could not base any products or advertising on future books, and had to always spread the gospel of Harry by drawing new consumers to his world. One guideline specifically stated that products should be 'artifacts rather than souvenirs,' when possible, i.e., if it's a broomstick, it should look like one Harry and his friends ride on while playing Quidditch."

According to some sources, one of the offshoots of Pottermania was the fact that numerous children began requesting eyeglasses that looked like the young wizard's.

The media had a field day depicting *Harry Potter and the Sorcerer's Stone* and Peter Jackson's *Lord of the Rings: Fellowship of the Ring* as arch rivals. According to Jackson himself, nothing could be further from the truth. "Everybody paints this sort of competition between *Harry Potter* and the *Lord of the Rings*. It's sort of crazy, because I just wish *Harry Potter* all the best and I'm sure it'll be great. I'm a huge fan of the books, so I'm looking forward to it."

Not surprisingly, all four Harry Potter novels jumped to the top of the UK bestseller lists shortly before the release of the film version of *Sorcerer's Stone*. Actually, the top five slots were all held by J.K. Rowling's creation, one of them being the movie tie-in version of the first novel. Bloomsbury Publishing enthused, "It is wonderful news and we are just delighted. It is quite funny to have the top five spots, considering there are only four Harry Potter stories so far. We couldn't have wished for better publicity from the film. Now people are rushing back to the bookshops to read the book first."

NBC aired a one-hour special entitled *Harry Potter: Behind the Magic*, a behind-the-scenes look at the film and its special effects.

Early in the process of shooting *Chamber of Secrets*, director Chris Columbus mentioned that he might be interested in shooting all seven Harry Potter films. Ultimately, though, he would decide

At the premiere of Harry Potter and the Sorcerer's Stone *in L.A., actors dressed as characters from the film greeted people on their way into the theater. (Frank Trapper/Corbis)*

that two was enough, in order to prevent further separation from his family.

Harry Potter and the Sorcerer's Stone opened to very positive reviews, though some complained that it followed the novel too closely and, for a film, that made for uneven pacing. Nonetheless, the film quickly went on to become a box office blockbuster all around the world. The film was made for $125 million. It had an opening domestic box office weekend gross of $90,294,621. It's total domestic gross was $317,575,550 and its foreign gross was $658,900,000, with a total worldwide gross of $976,475,550.

Members of London's Great Ormond Street Hospital claimed that the Harry Potter novels were aiding patients both physically and emotionally. Lisa Lewer, a clinical nurse, noted, "Harry Potter's predicaments are similar to the problems that face young people generally. Problems like dealing with the loss or separation from parents and family or the anxiety of forming new relationships in unfamiliar places. But the different ways Harry tackles them demonstrates to children that by exploring their own struggles they can often find ways of overcoming them."

One of the praises offered to the first film was that it felt thoroughly British, even to the point of using British terms that Americans might not get. Emphasized director Chris Columbus, "I vowed to make the film as British as possible. Did they redub *A Hard Day's Night*? Did they redub *A Man For All Seasons*? No, and we're not going to do it with this one."

Some American Harry fans were undaunted by the fact that *Sorcerer's Stone* opened in Britain a week before it did so in America, going so far as to fly overseas for a screening.

In an interview with the BBC, Chris Columbus revealed a bit of information about *Chamber of Secrets*, noting that they had shot sequences involving a flying car and a giant spider.

J.K. Rowling used her considerable clout to raise awareness and funds to help fight child poverty, particularly in one-parent families. Said Rowling, "Lone parents and their children are the poorest groups in our society. We are a wealthy nation, yet we have one of the worst records of child poverty in the industrialized world. It is a scandal."

Numerous interested parties had approached J.K. Rowling about stage rights to her novels, but the author has emphasized that she won't even entertain such offers until, at the very earliest, 2007. As her agent Christopher Little told the newspaper the *Stage*, "We have had requests every week from all over the world in connection with the stage rights to *Harry Potter and the Philosopher's Stone*. It would be difficult to give a figure, but it is in the hundreds."

Customs officers in Hong Kong arrested 10 people and charged them with bringing bootleg copies of *Harry Potter and the Sorcerer's Stone* into the country.

A Johannesburg, South Africa, woman named her newborn daughter after Hermione Granger.

The ABC television network announced that they had acquired the broadcast rights to *Sorcerer's Stone* and its sequels in a deal that would span 10 years.

CAST AND CREW INTERVIEWS FOR
HARRY POTTER AND THE SORCERER'S STONE

In time for the film's release, certain actors and filmmakers met with the press, and what follows are highlights from sessions with Robbie Coltrane,who plays Hagrid; director Chris Columbus; and the late Richard Harris, who originated the role of Professor Dumbledore.

ROBBIE COLTRANE
(Hagrid the Giant)

QUESTION: Children are going to be your biggest critics, right?
   COLTRANE: Absolutely. I got a letter from a woman the other day, and it started off very sweetly, "I've been a big fan of yours for X amount of years," and then, she said, "We're so glad that you're playing Hagrid because it's going to be very, very difficult to get that

blend between scariness and humor and millions of children throughout the world are relying on you." So, I thought, "No pressure there, then" [laughs], and of course, she was right.

QUESTION: Are they really tough with you on this one?
COLTRANE: Well no, it's their little world, you know. I have to treat it with respect.

QUESTION: How did they pull off the effect of making you appear to be a giant?
COLTRANE: I couldn't tell you that, because it would spoil the magic, you know. I mean, it's like Orson [Welles] says, "Everyone knows that the lady don't really get cut in two," and so, I'm leaving that one. It really would spoil it. If you knew, you would agree with me, trust me.

QUESTION: You mentioned achieving a balance. Was that really tough to do?
COLTRANE: No, it isn't, because you see, he is very scary. I mean, he's half a giant, and the giants aren't very nice as you will discover later on, and so, he has to have that edge to him, and they did it very cleverly. They said, when he kicks the door in and then says, "Sorry," I mean, that's the real Hagrid, do you know what I mean? He forgets how strong he is and he could break your neck with a snap of his finger.

QUESTION: Does it change the way you approach a character when people expect you to do it a certain way?
COLTRANE: [Laughs] No, not really. I mean, it was quite clear to me how the character should be played in the books and also, of course, Jo [Rowling] and I, we're great friends, we talked on the telephone for hours like a couple of adolescents about everything.

QUESTION: Like what?

Robbie Coltrane got the role of Hagrid, the lovable giant. (Diane Bondareff/ AP Photo)

COLTRANE: Well, the books are about everything. The books are about friendship and peer group pressure and how you discover your individuality and are you prepared to be unpopular and all those things that fuel your childhood, really. The magic, in a sense, is not really what they're about, I would suggest. That's the icing on the cake, I think.

QUESTION: What did J.K. Rowling reveal to you about Hagrid's character?

COLTRANE: Well, she said, "Imagine a Hell's Angel who gets off his Harley Davidson and comes into the part, but doesn't really move like in the biblical epic, you know, with the Red Sea." So, he starts with a cup of tea and talks about his garden — I thought that was great, because I have known people like that, but if you say anything rude about their garden, they will take you out and beat [you up], of course. That's Hagrid, really.

QUESTION: Was there a period where you had to determine the balance in Hagrid between humor and being serious?

COLTRANE: Well, it's quite clear, really, in the writing where he's supposed to be funny. I mean, Hagrid's problem is that when he starts talking, he doesn't know when to stop. He actually gives away the three major plotlines in here. So, that has to be an established part of his character, and otherwise, it just sounds like he's giving away plotlines, and so, he had to sound very natural, and that sort of became a bit of a catchphrase in the shooting because he does it about three times, and one of the things that I like about him is that he's not completely fearless. I think the fact that he calls that dog Fluffy is just hilarious.

QUESTION: Do you think this movie will be judged on two different standards?

COLTRANE: Oh absolutely, and children, as you know, are terrible sticklers for detail. They will know every single thing, and that's more scary for Chris [Columbus] than for anyone else.

QUESTION: Did you look like the Hagrid you imagined when you read the book?

COLTRANE: Yes, absolutely, and the makeup girls did a great job, they really did. That outfit weighed about sixty-five pounds.

QUESTION: Was it difficult to establish chemistry with the kids you were acting with?

COLTRANE: Not at all with these kids. I have to say the reason that actors don't like working with kids is because they don't have a very good emotional memory. If you say to them, "Imagine yourself at so and so, imagine when you were last really, really angry," and they have to be really, really angry fourteen times, and I mean, it's bad enough when you're an adult. So, what you do is that you always have fifteen takes with everything? It's the same with bloody animals — little Fluffy will only hit the mark once in forty takes. Then it's three in the morning and you want to go home, and so, they print the take that Fluffy hit the spot on, and you perhaps weren't very good in that take, and that's what that's about. But the kids were great. I have to say, as much as it goes against the grain to be nice about the director, Columbus is wonderful with children. Well, you can tell from seeing it. He really knows how to get the best out of them, because they were doing a lot of really subtle stuff, weren't they? Normally, kids in movies are either being cute or they're just being ghastly, aren't they? He managed to get all sorts of subtleties. You know, the way their friendships develop, and the way [Hermione] is sort of unlikable to start with, and then, you start to think, "Oh well, she's really alright," just like in the book. So, they were fine and they're proper children.

QUESTION: Did you get the sense from talking to J.K. Rowling that faithfulness to the book was important?

COLTRANE: Oh, absolutely. She got offered millions of pounds and you wouldn't believe the list of directors that wanted to do this who were turned down.

CHRIS COLUMBUS

(Director — *Sorcerer's Stone* and *Chamber of Secrets*)

QUESTION: Does criticism from the press affect you at all?

COLUMBUS: Actually, no, because I think that the movie speaks for itself. I initially didn't want to do a film like this because of the visual effects. I wasn't interested in working with the visual effects. But now, visual effects are at such a point where it's actually fun to work with them. My feeling has always been that you shouldn't let the effects overtake the story. I've seen it happen in so many films, where it's all about the effects, but our goal in *Harry* was to make it just like the book, about the characters. The effects are icing on the cake.

QUESTION: At what point did they ask you to do the second film?

COLUMBUS: It just seemed like a smooth transition, and I do remember in the initial conversation with Warner Brothers, they did say, "Could you do two back to back?" and I said, "I think so, as long as I get the editing worked out with the preproduction of the first" — we were editing while we were shooting, and so, I felt that I could do it. So, it was already in my mind anyway. I think they probably felt that, "Well, if he doesn't turn out to be a complete loss, we'll let him do two." I said to my cinematographer and production designer, "We need to push this film visually beyond anything that I've ever done." I said, "It has to be visually stunning, more than anything, more important than anything." Then I told the actors, "Your performances have to be incredibly real, naturalistic." My feeling, again, with Hogwarts and the whole world, it would have been easy to take this into some fantastical place that exists only in the imagination, but I felt when I read the books that Jo Rowling spoke to every eleven-year-old and said, "You know, you could potentially get a letter from Hogwarts School of Witchcraft and Wizardry." That gave these kids some hope in their lives and I thought, "That's what I want the film to be like," that you could actually, potentially get this letter. You want to make them believe in magic in a weird way, and I know that sounds corny, but it really is. You want kids to believe in the magic of it all.

QUESTION: Did these kids have any idea of what they were in store for in terms of the media's response to them?

COLUMBUS: Well, my initial feeling was that they shouldn't go to America and do things like Jay Leno or David Letterman; that they should remain slightly obscure. The good news is that they'll get to come back to England [to shoot the sequel] and get away from the publicity.

QUESTION: And you think Daniel Radcliffe will be able to handle the pressure?

COLUMBUS: In his case he's surrounded by two very strong, loving parents, and I think that they'll protect him.

QUESTION: In essence, do you think that's the difference between him and Macaulay Culkin?

COLUMBUS: Well, you know, I've had ten years away from that and I've learned from that experience. I learned as a director, again, like I said, you have to cast the parents; you have to see what kind of environment this kid lives in. You also have to realize that Dan really seems to love doing his work. I think that's one of the things that you look for as well — kids who are interested in the job, interested in being there and also, just that the parental relationship is a good one and a healthy one.

QUESTION: Are you saying that Macaulay didn't want to do the *Home Alone* films?

COLUMBUS: I don't know. I think that he was more interested, to be honest with you, in being a little kid and Dan has found a way to balance working and being a little kid, which I think is incredibly healthy.

QUESTION: Did you factor that in when you were holding auditions?

COLUMBUS: Yes, it was extremely important, and all of these kids were very real and very honest, and they hadn't done a lot of . . . well, Dan had done *David Copperfield*, obviously and about two seconds in *The Tailor of Panama*, but for the most part, most of the kids had never even been on a film set before. So, for me, that was important in terms of getting their performances to be real, because they don't come in with any sort of stage mothers or stage parents telling them how they should act. So, it's all very real — and psychologically, that's important; no stage mothers, no stage fathers. These kids come in and they realize that they're doing a job. British actors, I have found, and particularly even with the stars like Richard Harris and Maggie Smith, it's not about how big your trailer is, or, "Do I have a trainer, do I have a cook?" and all that star stuff that is so upsetting to me when I work in Hollywood sometimes.

QUESTION: How did you deal with making the movie as good as the book, as well as controlling the running time?

COLUMBUS: To me, it's a companion piece to the book. My goal was to involve Jo Rowling as a collaborator. People would say, "Well, isn't that going to interrupt your vision and isn't that going to get in the way of what you want this film to look like?" I thought, "If I were doing *Dracula* and I had access to Bram Stoker, I would certainly want to know what he was thinking." If I were doing a World War II movie, I would hire a consultant who had been in the war and who knew what was happening, in terms of reality. Jo was a very willing collaborator. She never came in with a sledgehammer and said, "This must be done this way, you need to do this." That never happened, and so, I just found it a joy to work with her. I'm being honest with you. It was four of us sitting in the room, and those were some of the best experiences that I had on this movie with Jo Rowling, Steve Kloves, David Heyman and myself. We laughed, we had fun, we talked about what would work on screen, what wouldn't work on screen; we got the script to where we wanted it to be; and we talked about the design and the look, and Jo was just a collaborator. Sometimes, we would say, "Well, how can we make this work? We need to change it from the book." A perfect example is the kids on the book cover who were wearing rugby shirts and jeans and sneakers with a wizard cloak over them. Well, we tested that look and it looked like a bad Halloween costume. So, we said to Jo, "Since this is steeped in British boarding school tradition, we need to get this to look like it exists in a real place," and that's why we came up with the uniforms, and she was all for that. I asked Jo at one point, "Do the kids wear wizard hats at all times?" and she said, "Yes, and most of them wear wizard hats through most of the book." I said,

"Well, I can't justify that. I think that it will start to feel a little odd if they wear wizard hats throughout the film. Can we just use wizard hats for special occasions, for the sword ceremony and the final piece?" and she agreed to that. So, that's the kind of conversations that you could have with Jo. She's never, never in your face, never gets in your way.

QUESTION: You decided to dramatize the opening monologue about how the baby shows up.

COLUMBUS: And she was fine with that. Actually, the initial opening of the film was a flashback to the death of Harry's parents, which Jo wrote for us. Well, we shot it and we realized that we should open the film with a bit of magic and slowly sort of lull the audience into the darkness, and the picture should get progressively darker as we get deeper into the film. So, we saved the death of Harry's parents for later.

QUESTION: Was there any concern about the fact it wasn't going to be a two-hour movie?

COLUMBUS: God no, I was hoping that it was going to be a three-hour movie, to be honest with you; but it's definitely not true that there was a four-hour cut. There was about a two-hour-and-forty-five minute cut but that was all we had. Then I tightened it up, paced it up a little and took it to Chicago with very crude visual effects, showed it to an audience because I wanted to get an opinion. Fifty percent Harry Potter fans and fifty percent nonreaders. I wanted to see if it was going to work from a character point of view. Anyway, the audience loved the movie — but the nonreaders loved the movie as much as the readers. The nonreaders said that they all wanted to go out and get the book, and the readers just loved it. The readers were like, "Well, this was missing and this was missing, but I still loved it," but the bottom line was that they all said it was too short. So, what I did was I put some things back and then I tightened the film up, and that's how it ended up at two hours and thirty-three minutes. I mean, that was the most shocking thing for me. I have to be honest with you, everyone who sees it, they seem to want more. People wanted to lose themselves in this world.

QUESTION: Why do you think that Harry Potter has struck such a nerve virtually everywhere?

COLUMBUS: I think that it really comes down to Jo's imagination. You know, I think that it really comes down to the fact that she has tapped into something emotional and magical about kids, and I do think that they really want to believe in magic. Some of the questions for the kids at a press conference were, "Do you believe in magic?" Well, no one really believes in people who fly around on broomsticks. It's like the guy who said that they were flying the wrong way on broomsticks. I said, "Well, if one of these 'witches' wants to fly up to me the right way on a broomstick, I'll redo the shot." But yeah, I think that it's the belief that magic and hope can potentially exist in your life. You know, I think that you get that in the book, obviously, in a non-sentimental way and a really straightforward way that touches people.

RICHARD HARRIS
(Professor Dumbledore)

QUESTION: Did you enjoy making this film?

HARRIS: Well, I enjoyed seeing it more than I enjoyed making it. I enjoyed watching it, and I think that it was great. We had a whole bunch of kids there yesterday. They were children too young to go to the premiere, who were kind of my godchildren and they sat through it, and I said, "Was it too long?" and they said, no, they could have done another hour. It was unbelievable.

Richard Harris originally turned down the part of Dumbledore, until his grand-daughter threatened to stop speaking to him if he didn't take the role. (Max Nash/AP Photo)

QUESTION: Was the shooting difficult?

> **HARRIS:** It's difficult, because you only have so many hours a day to work with the kids. The laws here are very strict, and quite rightly so. So when your turn comes to perform, they watch you and tell you that you have an hour to do it, because the kids are back in an hour. So, you have to get in and get it done quick; but yeah, I enjoyed it. It's a wonderful job for a guy my age.

QUESTION: Are children challenging to work with?

> **HARRIS:** They're marvelous, and I'll tell you what happened. When Christopher Columbus, the director, asked me to come down and meet the kids, I met Ron [Rupert Grint] and Dan [Radcliffe] and

Emma [Watson], and I kind of hung around them for a couple of hours to get to know them. And then, Chris Columbus asked me if I would mind reading with them, doing scenes with them, and I said, "Sure." So, we played all the scenes, all the scenes that we had to play together, and when it was all finished, Rupert looked at me and he said, "That was quite a good reading that you gave. I think that you'll be okay in this part." An eleven-year-old!

QUESTION: How much Dumbledore came from the book and how much came from discussions with Chris Columbus?

HARRIS: I just talked to Chris and I said, "I know what I'm going to do," and that was to find a voice, because there are no references. I mean, he has no scenes, in this picture anyway, except with the boy, and they're just lectures. There are no acting exchanges between me and the kids in the picture. All he's doing is lecturing and giving speeches.

QUESTION: Would you say that kids are going to be your biggest critics?

HARRIS: Oh, you bet your ass. A young girl, yesterday, she was the daughter of a journalist that I had to give an interview to, and she was at the picture in the afternoon, and Molly was her name, and she was sitting there, and I said, "What did you think, Molly?" She said, "I liked it, it's good, but of course, it wasn't called the Dark Forest, it's called the Forbidden Forest in the book," and she's only about nine. Then she said, "Hermione, she's all wrong," and I said, "What do you mean?" "Well, she's supposed to have buckteeth." These kids know every single thing about that book and if you put a finger wrong, boy, they jump on you. They wanted to know, some of the kids that were there from my family, the young ones, eight, nine and ten, they said, "Well, your beard was slightly wrong," and I said, "What?" They said, "Well, your beard was supposed to be under your belt." Critics.

QUESTION: Why do you think Harry Potter has taken off the way that it has?

HARRIS: I'm afraid that I don't know. All I know is that my grand-daughter — and this is a legendary story now, and so I'm only repeating what's been in the press before — but when they wanted me to do it, originally, I didn't want to do it. And the reason that I didn't was not because of the quality of it or the content of it, it's because you had to commit your life. I mean, if they're going to make seven movies, I've got to do them, that was it. There was no way out of it, and I hate commitment. I loath it, I loath having dates and I hate having to be someplace. Like, I hate having to be here, which really doesn't matter. So, the point really is that the idea that my life has now been controlled, if they make seven, and they're certainly going to make three, maybe even four, and the idea that your life is controlled by that doesn't suit me at all. I hate that.

QUESTION: So why did you do it?

HARRIS: Because my granddaughter called me up and said, "Poppa, if you don't play Dumbledore, I will never speak to you again." So I hung up, called my agent and said, "Okay, I'll do it. I can't afford to lose that gig." But having said that, I'm glad that I did it because when you get to seventy years of age, parts don't come in all that easy. I mean, all the right parts for seventy-year-olds, enough of them, and it's a wonderful project and it's a wonderful part. I just have to condition myself to the fact that I've got to do more.

December 2001

Bridget Jones's Diary costar Shirley Henderson was cast as the ghost Moaning Myrtle in *Harry Potter and the Chamber of Secrets.*

J.K. Rowling with her husband, Neil Murray. (John D McHugh/AP Photo)

In an interview with the BBC, J.K. Rowling revealed that she had written the last chapter of the seventh and final Harry Potter novel. "This really wraps everything," she said. "It's the epilogue and I basically say what happens to everyone after they leave school, those who survive — because there are deaths, more deaths coming."

There was an intention to turn the train used as the Hogwarts Express into a tourist attraction, but those plans were . . . derailed . . . by Warner Brothers' lawyers.

J.K. Rowling celebrated Christmas day by marrying Dr. Neil Murray. This was her second marriage.

Casting rumors for the third Harry film, *Prisoner of Azkaban*: Ewan McGregor as Remus Lupin and Robson Green as Sirius Black. As it turns out, the rumors were false.

The success of *Harry Potter and the Sorcerer's Stone* had a positive effect on sales of the novel it was based on (not that they needed the boost): the first novel sold 1.1 million copies in England, which was over 200,000 more than *Goblet of Fire*.

Maggie Smith was enthusiastic to a *USA Today* reporter in pointing out that Kenneth Branagh would be appearing in *Chamber of Secrets*. "Ken Branagh plays this rather glamorous teacher who comes in. I love the idea that the detention [the children] have to do after school if they've misbehaved is to answer all his fan mail."

January 2002

When the Producers Guild of America announced their nominations, *Harry Potter and the Sorcerer's Stone* was nominated in the category of the Darryl F. Zanuck Producer of the Year Award, going up against *A Beautiful Mind*, *Fellowship of the Ring*, *Moulin Rouge* and *Shrek* (*Moulin Rouge* took the prize).

In an interview with A&E's *Biography*, J.K. Rowling discussed the fact that at least one major character would die in upcoming novels. "Death is an extremely important theme throughout all seven books," she said. "Possibly the most important theme. If you are writing about evil — which I am, I'm writing about someone who is essentially a psychopath — you have a duty to show the real evil of taking a human life. More people are going to die."

February 2002

Warner Brothers announced that *Sorcerer's Stone* would be making its DVD debut on May 28.

Jason Isaacs was signed to play Draco Malfoy's father, Lucius, in *Chamber of Secrets*. The actor enthused, "This character is as odious a character as I've ever read, and so this year I'll be despised by children the globe over." Elsewhere he added, "It's my first film about wizards, and I don't get to wear waist-length blond hair and walk around with a snake-headed cane very often. For me, the fun and challenge of playing this character was making Lucius as grotesque as I could, but somehow keeping him real. Lucius is a very dark character and a thoroughly unpleasant man. He's the most confident person I've ever stepped inside and completely supreme in his arrogance and ruthlessness. He is pure evil."

A first edition of *The Philosopher's Stone* went up for auction in London, and was won for a bid of approximately $15,000 U.S.

In its final global box office tally, *Harry Potter and the Sorcerer's Stone* became the second highest-grossing film of all time (behind James Cameron's *Titanic*). As a result, *Star Wars Episode One: The Phantom Menace* got nudged down to third place.

March 2002

Twenty-three-year-old Christian Coulson was cast as Tom Riddle, essentially a younger version of Harry Potter's ultimate enemy, Lord Voldemort. Other casting for *Chamber of Secrets* included Miriam Margolyes as Professor Sprout, Mark Williams as Ron Weasley's father, Gemma Jones as Madam Pomfrey and Sally Mortemore as Madam Pince.

J.K. Rowling took legal steps to stop a Swedish radio station from broadcasting excerpts from her novels. Noted a spokesperson,

"Our policy is that the Harry Potter series only be broadcast in their unabridged version to protect the integrity of the books."

John Cleese expressed his pleasure at returning as the ghost Nearly Headless Nick in *Chamber of Secrets*. "I think my participation is going to be minimal," he said, "but I'm still extremely happy to be part of it. The kids are just wonderful."

Bloomsbury Publishing announced that there was no official publication date for book five, *Harry Potter and the Order of the Phoenix*. Said a spokesman, "She's still writing it. Until she delivers the manuscript, we won't announce a publication date. We're hoping it will be this autumn. It probably will be later in the fall."

Harry Potter and the Sorcerer's Stone found itself nominated for nine Saturn Awards.

April 2002

A number of Siberian children became sick when they ingested a "Harry Potter Magic Potion" keychain that included copper sulphate. In response, Hallmark, who manufactured the item in the United States, recalled 7,000 units. Explained the Associated Press, "The product includes a "potion bottle" filled with purple-colored mineral oil and red-colored water. It contains petroleum distillate, a fuel-burning substance that can cause breathing problems and become fatal if breathed into the lungs, a safety commission spokeswoman said. Hallmark recalled the three-inch key chain voluntarily. The product is made of styrene and has a green base, a gold top and the letters 'HP' printed on the bottle."

Video stores were making preparations for the arrival of *Harry Potter and the Sorcerer's Stone* on DVD.

May 2002

Once Chris Columbus made it clear that he had no intention of directing *Harry Potter and the Prisoner of Azkaban*, Warner Brothers began looking for a successor and found it with Alfonso Cuaron, whose credits include the coming-of-age drama, *Y Tu Mamá También*.

Publication of *Harry Potter and the Order of the Phoenix* was announced for June 2003.

June 2002

Addressing children at the Guardian Hay festival, a Warner Brothers executive let slip how they make Hagrid a giant. According to Tanya Seghatchian, there are two Hagrids (one a stand-in), and two sets, one smaller than the other, to create the illusion.

July 2002

Forty-one-year-old Melissa Kumsuk Cho was deported from the United Kingdom once it was confirmed that she had been stalking J.K. Rowling.

The official announcement was made that Alfonso Cuaron would be directing film number three, *Harry Potter and the Prisoner of Azkaban*, with Chris Columbus taking on the role of producer. Said Cuaron, "I am so pleased to be entrusted with presenting the continuing Harry Potter saga. It has captured the imagination of so many people, myself included, and I am so excited to join an amazingly talented cast and crew."

August 2002

It was a quiet month in the Potterverse, except that J.K. Rowling was battling with her neighbors. For reasons of security, she wanted to increase the height of the walls around her estate. Ultimately, Rowling got her way.

September 2002

Some people in the media worried that Daniel Radcliffe was aging too quickly to keep playing Harry Potter. Noted the *Sunday Mail*, "He may be getting too big for his broomstick. Daniel Radcliffe, who played the boy wizard in the film *Harry Potter and the Philosopher's Stone* last year, appears to be outgrowing the role. Seen walking to a gym near their home in southwest London, 13-year-old Daniel is easily taller than his mother Marcia Gresham. . . . Filming of the second J.K. Rowling adventure, *Harry Potter and the Chamber of Secrets*, was rushed through after the first movie to reduce the risk of any of the child actors growing up too much. If Daniel's dizzy rise continues at the same rate, director Christopher Columbus may be forced to look for a replacement wizard for future Potter films."

While filming *Chamber of Secrets*, Chris Columbus gave an interview in which he stated, "What's great about the books is they're not really sequels, they're individual stories about the next year at Hogwarts School of Witchcraft and Wizardry. So as a result, you get to examine each of the characters as they continue to grow. This time around, the kids are starting to experience those first feelings of adolescence and developing small little crushes here and there. The characters are becoming slightly more complex, and that will continue more and more as we get deeper in the series."

Rowling received word that the United States court system had dismissed Nancy Stouffer's claim that Rowling's works were inspired by her *Legend of Rah and the Muggles*.

It was announced that Rowling and her husband, Dr. Neil Murray, were expecting their first child together in the spring.

Educational publishers Kumon published the results of a survey in which *Harry Potter and the Philosopher's Stone* was deemed the best children's story of all time.

Warner Brothers announced that *Chamber of Secrets* would have its world premiere in London on November 3.

October 2002

Sad news: It was announced that actor Richard Harris, who had enchanted audiences with his portrayal of Professor Dumbledore, was battling cancer, although he was expected to reprise his role for the third time in *Prisoner of Azkaban*. By the end of the month, however, Harris had passed away.

In an interview with Sci Fi Wire, Chris Columbus revealed that J.K. Rowling's involvement with the films had been minimal, due to the fact that she basically trusted those involved. "Jo was involved with the script again," he said. "As always, she has a lot of information that none of us have, in terms of where the characters are going and in terms of what's going to happen to them. She's also got the backgrounds of all these characters in this world in hundreds of notebooks. So we can basically call her or email her and find out any little piece of information we need. That relationship still exists. I think she trusts us a lot, so her involvement this time was actually a little less than on the first film."

Chris Columbus mused that the young cast of the Harry Potter films — Daniel Radcliffe, Emma Watson and Rupert Grint — would leave their roles following the third film. Obviously he was wrong.

November 2002

Web site www.harrypotter.co.uk announced that it would be broadcasting over the Internet the London premiere of *Chamber of Secrets* straight from the red carpet.

Speaking to the *Detroit Free Press*, director Chris Columbus expressed his feelings about moving immediately from the release of *Sorcerer's Stone* to *Chamber of Secrets*. "It was the weirdest feeling," he admitted. "Because on one hand I was exhausted, and on the other I felt completely relaxed. I felt that with the first movie we had earned the fans' trust, we had earned J.K. Rowling's trust, we had earned Warner Brothers' trust and the pressure was off. Now all we had to be concerned with was making the best movie we could from the second book. It was like the pressure of the first date was over and now we could get on with the relationship." In the same interview he described some of the differences, from his point of view, between the two films. "With *Chamber of Secrets* I had nine months to get the effects right. The kids were stronger in their roles, feeling more like they owned them instead

By Chamber of Secrets, *Daniel Radcliffe had become an undeniable star.*
(David Bebber/Reuters/Corbis)

of just borrowing them. The whole cast was like a family. I had decided to use a lot of handheld camera on this one, which gave us all a huge sense of freedom. But the biggest benefit was that we were able to head right into the story, without explaining everything. It was more like, 'Hold on, here we go!'"

On that same subject, producer David Heyman added, "It was challenging. Fortunately we benefited from the experience of the first film and having many of our original production crew continue on through the second film, so we had a wealth of knowledge to draw upon."

In an interview, Columbus revealed one of the benefits of going right into production while *Sorcerer's Stone* was just hitting theaters: "None of us had the chance to sit back and think about the success of the first film, which I think was good for everyone, particularly the kids. By that point, the cast and crew had become like one big family. It was great that we could all share that sense of excitement, without losing our momentum, and carry it into *Chamber of Secrets*."

In an interview with CBS *The Early Show*, Daniel Radcliffe addressed the experience of shooting *Chamber of Secrets*: "I'm getting more and more into my part, and it's getting kind of harder to differentiate between me [and Harry], 'cause as time goes on, I'm finding more things that connect us both. When reading the fourth book, you find out even more things we share. It's really weird."

Verso Books, the publisher of *The Irresistible Rise of Harry Potter* by Andrew Blake, was forced to pull the book from bookstores due to the fact that J.K. Rowling's lawyers felt its dust jacket design gave the impression that it was an officially sanctioned book.

While speaking to the BBC, Daniel Radcliffe noted, "I love English at school — that's what I really love. I love reading and just writing and everything, so I think I might like to be a writer [instead of an actor]. Or, because I was given, like, a love of film by Chris Columbus, I think I might like to be a director."

The *Toledo Blade* reported that the success of the Harry Potter films had actually had an impact on British tourism. "With a second Harry Potter movie just opening in the United States, the British tourism industry hopes to capitalize on the great popularity of J.K. Rowling's creation by marketing the United Kingdom as a land of owls and ghosts, giants and enchanted forests. Promoting Harry Potter's 'magical Britain' became part of a campaign to encourage more international visitors after foot-and-mouth disease and 9/11 caused visits to the United Kingdom to drop by nine percent in 2001. When the first movie came out in November of last year, the British Tourism Authority published a 'movie map' highlighting sites from the films and books, while tour organizers scrambled to

The Glenfinnan Viaduct in Scotland was used as the track that takes the wizards-in-training from Platform 9¾ to Hogwarts. (Fionna Boyle)

put together itineraries with Harry Potter themes. The reaction was immediate and tremendous. The Tourist Authority began receiving nine times as many visitors to their Web site and more than 200 calls a day on their 'Hedwig Hotline'."

Harry Potter and the Chamber of Secrets got generally positive reviews from the critics, and boffo box office numbers. The film, made at a cost of $100 million (actually $25 million *less* than its predecessor, which is highly unusual for a sequel), had an opening weekend gross in north America of $88,357,488. In the end it would have a domestic take of $261,988,482 and a foreign gross of $615,700,000, totaling $877,688,482 worldwide. All told, the film did about $100 million less than *Harry Potter and the Sorcerer's Stone*.

Both David Heyman and Chris Columbus shared their views that this film represented a further evolution in Harry Potter's saga, just as the novel had. Said Heyman, "We devoted a good part of *Sorcerer's Stone* to setting up the world of Harry Potter. There was so much to introduce in terms of the magic, the settings and the characters. With *Chamber of Secrets*, Harry exudes a lot more confidence and strength right from the start." Added Columbus, "*Chamber of Secrets* is darker and funnier and it takes Harry's character to a new place. The first film was about Harry realizing that he's actually a wizard. In contrast to the color and larger-than-life characters that surrounded him, Harry was somewhat passive and didn't come into his own until the third act of the film."

Daniel Radcliffe revealed that he felt a connection to Harry's growth as a character. "He had developed so much," said Radcliffe, "I had to develop myself, too, and now I have two instincts — Harry's and my own. So when we were filming each scene, I asked myself, 'How would Harry react to this?' and I tried to get that feeling across on screen." Added Columbus, "Daniel took on an enormous responsibility when he was cast to play Harry Potter, and he has risen to the challenge and totally matured as an actor. He's become a real leading man in the truest sense of the word, as well as becoming a real hero and probably a bit of a heartthrob."

Daniel Radcliffe was not the only recipient of praise from the filmmakers. Of Rupert Grint and Emma Watson, Columbus enthused, "It's remarkable to see how far they've grown, not just physically but in their acting. The kids' performances are more mature and, quite frankly, they are even better than they were in the first film." Heyman concurred, "One of the wonders of this process for me has been to witness the maturation of Dan, Rupert and Emma. The children seem more confident and able to draw upon a wealth of new experience for their characters. Yet at the same time, they have maintained their enthusiasm, sense of wonder and their youthfulness."

Harry Potter and the Chamber of Secrets brought with it a number of visual effects challenges, which the filmmakers discussed at the time of release. Chris Columbus offered high praise for visual effects supervisors Jim Mitchell and Nick Davis. "With Jim and Nick," he said, "we found a team that really understands what I call the reality of visual effects. They understand our desire to transport people to a place they've never been before, but at the same time, make certain that they absolutely believe what they are seeing." One challenge for the film was the creation of Dobby the House Elf, a computer-generated creature. Said Columbus, "I wanted Dobby to be a character that felt very real and it's one that the audience would fall in love with. Jim and Nick created an adorable character who feels like he genuinely inhabits this special world."

The giant spider Aragog presented another challenge, as Nick Dudman from the film's creature department detailed: "We were asked to create a walking, talking nine-foot spider with an 18-foot leg span. Each leg had to be manipulated by a different team member, and the whole contraption operated on a complex combination of aquatronics [underwater pneumatic air rams] and a series of computers with video monitors. The entire creature weighed three quarters of a ton." Of Aragog, Daniel Radcliffe enthused, "I remember the first shot we did in the Spider's Hollow. Rupert and I went over this ledge and suddenly there's a gigantic spider waiting for us. It was so realistic, we were both genuinely terrified."

At the time of *Harry Potter and the Chamber of Secrets'* release, a press conference was held featuring Daniel Radcliffe, Rupert Grint and Emma Watson. Chris Columbus met with the press as well. What follows are edited transcripts of those sessions.

DANIEL RADCLIFFE, EMMA WATSON AND RUPERT GRINT

(Harry Potter, Hermione Granger, and Ron Weasley)

QUESTION: There's a line in this movie that Kenneth Branagh says: celebrity is as celebrity does. You guys are all celebrities now. What's the last year been like for you? Is there a good story you can tell?

> **DANIEL RADCLIFFE:** The best thing so far for me was at the premiere [of *Harry Potter and the Sorcerer's Stone* in London], where I met Ben Stiller. That was really cool. And then I went to the New York premiere and I met Tim Robbins and Susan Sarandon. So that's probably been the best bit so far.
>
> **RUPERT GRINT:** Getting recognized is pretty cool. One time I got recognized up a mountain, when I went to Switzerland. That was cool.
>
> **EMMA WATSON:** Probably the best thing is going to really, really cool premieres and getting to pick really cool outfits.

QUESTION: Daniel, Chris Columbus said that you'd developed as a leading man, a hero and even a bit of a heartthrob since the first film. Do you feel like a heartthrob, and do you have girls coming up to you now?

> **DANIEL:** Personally, I can't actually see it, but if other people can, great.

QUESTION: Can each of you pick one thing that you think will happen to your characters later on in the books?

> **EMMA:** She will be something really clever. She'll be a doctor or something. She'll be really academic in her job.
>
> **DANIEL:** Does it have to be about my character? I think these two (Hermione and Ron) are going to get together. That's my prediction.
>
> **RUPERT:** I was going to say I hope (Hermione and Ron) *don't* fall for each other.

QUESTION: Can you describe the kind of fan mail you get? Are any of the letters particularly funny or do they creep you out?

    DANIEL: I'm just amazed at the amount of effort [that's put into the letters]. Around my birthday time I got lots of presents. Just the effort that was put into them was unbelievable. It's so amazing.

    EMMA: For my birthday someone gave me a massive, big, white cuddly bear about as big as me. They sent it in a post to me. I just think that was completely amazing if they've never met me. It was just really weird.

    RUPERT: It was my sister's birthday and somebody got her something as well.

QUESTION: Chris Columbus won't be directing *Prisoner of Azkaban*. Are you excited about having a new director or are you a little nervous?

    DANIEL: I think the most important thing to mention is that Chris is still going to be around. He's going to be the producer, so he's still going to be there. I think with the new director it's going to be exciting and it's going to be a different and a new experience.

    EMMA: Daniel said everything I want to say. But Chris is still going to be there, so it's not like he's going forever. Alfonso [Cuaron] is a really, really nice guy and I think it's really exciting to be working with somebody new as well.

    RUPERT: I'm going to miss Chris as well, but he's always going to be around and Alfonso is really good.

QUESTION: This movie has more action and it's darker than *Sorcerer's Stone*. Do you think some younger kids will be frightened by some of the scenes, like the spider sequence?

    DANIEL: I personally don't think so. It's all in the book and if you take away the darkness from the film, then you haven't done the book justice. And so, if they've read the book, I don't think they'll be scared of it at all.

    EMMA: I think the fans will be really, really happy with it. I think [for younger viewers] it just depends on the parents.

Emma, Daniel and Rupert do the press interviews for Chamber of Secrets.
(Suzanne Plunkett/AP Photo)

RUPERT: It's pretty scary. And as Emma said, it's up to the parents if they want to put their child through that.

QUESTION: What's the best thing and worst thing about playing these characters?

DANIEL: I think the best thing, without a doubt, is playing a character that has inspired children all over the world — and adults. Honestly, I don't think there is a worst thing.

EMMA: It's the acting, which I really, really enjoyed. Even when you take away the glamor and attention and premieres and everything, it still comes down to the fact that you're acting. [It was also great to] be with fantastic directors, actors and just the people I worked with.

RUPERT: For me it was coughing up slugs and coming to New York. Both were the best.

QUESTION: What did you do during down-time on set with each other?

RUPERT: We did loads of funny stuff. I just can't remember any of them.

DANIEL: When we weren't filming I just basically locked myself up in a very small room and watched films.

EMMA: When I'm not filming, I'm at school and I play lots of sports, do a lot of art and hang out with my friends most of the time.

QUESTION: Daniel, in the second film Harry comes back to Hogwarts as a sort of a celebrity based on his achievements in the first film. That's both good and bad for the character and his life at school. Does your own life reflect that experience at all? When you went back to school were you liked or disliked by some people because you were famous?

DANIEL: I've moved schools. All the people that I've met have been absolutely fantastic. There's no jealousy. I haven't been bullied or anything. Everybody's been really nice.

QUESTION: The three of you seem to be such great kids, but have you guys ever had a fight? Did Chris ever have to come in, be referee, say "Make up; it'll be better tomorrow"?

DANIEL: I threw Rupert through a window. . . . No. We've never had a fight.

QUESTION: You're all at an age where changes are happening rapidly. When you're acting, does Chris want you to play younger or do you just play your age?

EMMA: [We] play our age, I think. It's great. It's like we're growing up with the books. We're the same age as [the characters], so we're kind of growing up with them.

QUESTION: How did the experience of filming the first *Harry Potter* affect you this time around? Did it give you more confidence?

DANIEL: I felt I was certainly a lot more confident with Chris. If I had an idea I was more comfortable talking to him about it, whereas on the first one I wouldn't have been able to do that.

RUPERT: I was a bit more comfortable because we knew from the first one what everything was [going to be like]. We knew about the scheduling and everything.

EMMA: I think everyone was a lot more confident and a lot more comfortable because we all knew the crew and we knew the director and we knew what we were doing for starters, which was good. I just think everybody came back feeling a lot more confident.

QUESTION: Would you all like to continue on with the series, doing all seven? Or do you want to go off and have a normal life?

EMMA: I don't even know if they're going to make a fourth or a fifth film or whatever. But it's been a really, really good experience and I've really enjoyed them. So, yeah, I suppose.

DANIEL: I'm definitely doing the third film. We're all doing the third film. After that, who knows? It takes more or less a year to film (each movie), so we've got quite a long way before we have to encounter that decision.

RUPERT: I've really enjoyed doing them all.

QUESTION: A special effects question for each of you. Emma, can you talk about being petrified? Daniel, can you tell us about the climactic battle with the snake? And Rupert, can you talk about coughing up slugs?

EMMA: There was this amazing wax model of me [looking petrified]. I had to have a whole [body cast] made of me. I didn't have to actually lie down like this [looks stiff] for a half hour.

DANIEL: In the books, the basilisk is supposed to be 80 feet long, I think. They built 25 feet of it, including the head, which was actually quite hard to fight. I kept knocking the teeth out of the mouth, so they had to spend endless hours repairing it.

RUPERT: The slugs scene was probably my favorite, because I had to try out all these different flavored slimes. There was orange, lemon, peppermint, chocolate and it made it taste really nice. I really enjoyed it!

QUESTION: How are your families dealing with your fame?

DANIEL: My parents are really amazing because they've helped me with absolutely everything that I've done. I couldn't have done anything like this without them.

RUPERT: My parents have helped me keep my feet on the ground.

EMMA: My parents, I think, have been really, really supportive.

QUESTION: Which scenes for *Azkaban* are you three most excited to shoot and which scene — dramatic scene as opposed to effects scene — in *Chamber of Secrets* were you most excited to shoot?

> **EMMA:** I'm really looking forward to flying on the hippogriff. My favorite scene from this movie was probably the Gilderoy Lockhart scene. I thought that was pretty good.
>
> **DANIEL:** In the third film I think I'm really looking forward to doing all the stuff with Lupin and Sirius Black, with those characters. In this film, I loved filming the dueling scene because there was a huge crowd in there and I love all the scenes with loads of people, and plus, having Ken Branagh and Alan Rickman together was fantastic to watch.
>
> **RUPERT:** My favorite scene in this film was the flying car, because that was just wicked. And in the third film I'm looking forward to meeting one of the dementors.

QUESTION: If you could really do magic, what's the one spell you'd most like to cast?

> **RUPERT:** I'd like to have the flying car. I think that would be really cool.
>
> **DANIEL:** I'd like to have the invisibility cloak because if you get into trouble, then you can just run off very, very fast in the opposite direction.
>
> **EMMA:** I would like to have an invisibility cloak, too.

QUESTION: You had two new actors working on this film, Jason Isaacs and Kenneth Branagh. Can you talk a little bit about working with them and did you do anything to initiate them into the group?

> **DANIEL:** It was amazing working with Jason Isaacs and Kenneth Branagh. Not only are they two of the most fantastic actors, but they're two of the nicest people. So far as initiation, there was nothing that I know of.

EMMA: They are two of the most fantastic actors on the set, and off the set they're two of the nicest guys ever. They're the funniest guys I've met as well.

RUPERT: I was a bit nervous about meeting them at first. But they're just really nice people, really down to earth and funny.

QUESTION: You guys have given three years of your lives to this film series so far. What's been the most satisfying aspect of it all? Is it the attention? Is it acting? Is it meeting the people?

RUPERT: It's meeting the people. It's going to places like New York. It's coughing up slugs. And it's seeing the final [version of the film]. That's really good.

DANIEL: I think one of the best things is actually seeing the finished product, like Rupert said. You work on it for 10 months and then you finally see it, and it's a really great moment when you actually see it all completed.

EMMA: You guys nicked my answer. You spend 10 months doing it, but you haven't seen the special effects. You haven't seen the editing. You haven't seen anything. So it's this massive surprise when you see it. That's really, really rewarding.

QUESTION: What do you each identify with most in the characters you're playing? And has that carried over into your real life at all?

EMMA: In my real life I don't go around saying "Holy cricket" too much. Sometimes I find myself saying some of the lines from the film, but not very often.

DANIEL: I think I'm going to have to go and have therapy one day because when I keep reading the books I just find out more about myself that Harry has in his personality, too, like curiosity, loyalty, not being afraid to stand up for yourself, getting in trouble.

RUPERT: When I was reading the books I was starting to relate to Ron because we're kind of similar. We both have ginger hair. We both are scared of spiders. We both have quite a big family and we both like sweets.

QUESTION: You guys will be 75 years old, in your rockers and still known as the Harry Potter children. Is there a downside to that?

> **DANIEL:** If I do go on to act or whatever I do do, I think I'll try to separate myself from the character. At the same time, it's not something I'll ever be ashamed of. This is a huge achievement and something to be proud of.

> **EMMA:** I think I could be 100 years old and be in my rocker, but I'll always be very, very proud to say that I was in the Harry Potter films.

> **RUPERT:** Yeah, me too.

QUESTION: Daniel, this character has a dark side to him in this film. What did you learn from that?

> **DANIEL:** I think everybody has a dark side, really. However much you show it or whether you're afraid to show it, I think everybody has it. So it was great to be able to show Harry's dark side. It was just great to be able to show that he's not flawless, he's not the perfect person.

QUESTION: Daniel, how did you work with Dobby, especially since the character wasn't really there to act with?

> **DANIEL:** It wasn't quite not there. There was an orange ball on a stick, which helps. Because the actual creature is so animated and jumping all over the place it's quite hard to actually get a fix on where it is at one time. But it was made so easy by everybody around us that we got used to it.

CHRIS COLUMBUS
(Director)

QUESTION: You've got four children. The word is that you've chosen not to direct *Harry Potter and the Prisoner of Azkaban* in order to spend more time with your family. True?

> **COLUMBUS:** They're the people who got me into it and, ironically, the people who are getting me out. My daughter Eleanor was the person who forced me to read the books and told me it would make a great movie. And then I realized after two and a half years of not seeing them for dinner during the week that I wanted to take them to school in the morning and see them for dinner. So that's why I'm not doing the third movie.

QUESTION: How tough is it for you, on the professional side, to walk away from this franchise?

> **COLUMBUS:** It's tough, but honestly, about halfway through *Chamber of Secrets* I was putting everything — blood, sweat and tears — into the thing. I was performing with the kids. It was insane. I thought, physically, that I don't think I could do a third. It's not like sitting on a set with Susan Sarandon, Julia Roberts or even Robin Williams and Ed Harris [saying], "Okay, can you bring it down a little?" as I sit back in the director's chair. This is not like that. This is completely interactive directing. I thought, "I'll die of a heart attack if I do the third film." It's just too intense. Directing Dan sword fighting one day I thought, "This is not a way for a 43-year-old man to make a living," but I had such fun and it kept me energetic and exciting and going. But I do need about a year to just sort of recharge. I couldn't give back to the kids in a third movie what I gave them in the first two movies.

A visitor looks at a wax figure of Dobby during a traveling exhibition from St. Petersburg's wax figure museum. (Petar Petrov/AP Photo)

QUESTION: How did the kids react when you told them you'd not direct the third film?

    COLUMBUS: I told them all separately. And they each took it differently. Dan was probably the most disappointed. Emma is tough and she knew, "Okay, I'm going to go on." But they were all concerned that I wasn't going to just pack up and leave. I promised them; I reassured them that I would be on the set as a producer, making the transition work with the new director. We have a very comfortable set. It's like a family. It's a loving set. The kids can do what they want and feel secure, and I feel that part of it is just because we've created this atmosphere of no adults screaming at each other. It's not tension-filled at all. If there's any concern or conflict it goes off the set. And I want to make sure that continues. If I see any of that stuff, whoever does it will be out the door in a second.

QUESTION: Technically, what was the toughest sequence to pull off?

    COLUMBUS: The toughest was Dobby. The basilisk was fun to shoot. That was one day we just threw out the storyboards and decided to really have a lot of fun. We took the camera off the tripod with the basilisk. But with Dobby, Dan basically had to focus on a green [*sic*] ball at the end of a stick. The first day was a little difficult, and then he got into it. Even in the dailies, where you saw him interacting with this green ball, you realized, "God, it feels like there's someone else there," even though Dobby wasn't in the frame yet. The animators at ILM [Industrial Light and Magic] said they'd never seen any actor do it as well as Dan. They said they've had actors twice his age who haven't been able to focus. But he makes those scenes work really well. We also wanted the character of Dobby, because he is CG, not to have this certain curse of another CGI I won't reveal. This guy was so annoying and he scared the hell out of us.

QUESTION: How much does a Potter movie feel like a big Hollywood movie and how much does it feel like a little British movie when you've got these respected British actors?

    COLUMBUS: It never feels like a Hollywood movie. That's what's great about being in England. You've got these stars — Maggie Smith and Richard Harris. There is ego, but they're there to work. It's all about the work, so there aren't trailers and cooks and trainers and all of that nonsense. Also, I think I've seen every one of them on the West End. They need to do theater and it's not a step down for them to do TV. So they're constantly working. There is none of that Hollywood stuff. And the kids themselves did the (U.S.) premiere last year, did Letterman and Leno, and then the movie opened on a Friday. Three days later they were shooting *Chamber of Secrets*. So they didn't even have time to be affected by all of this. And going back to England is different. Even though the press there is pretty savage, they've stayed away from the kids. They'll follow Victoria Beckham and those people around the streets forever, but for some reason they've left the kids alone. I think that in two years there's only been one photograph of Dan in the newspaper, walking with his mother. They got a couple of other photographs of stand-ins and stuff. So they've been kind to the kids, which is great.

Director Chris Columbus noticed that Emma Watson, along with her other two co-stars, had become much more comfortable in front of the camera by the second film. (John D McHugh/AP Photo)

QUESTION: How has Dan changed since this all began?

    COLUMBUS: He's not changed personally. He's kind of becoming more of a leading man. He's got more confidence as an actor, which I think is pretty obvious from the film. As a person, he still thanks me after a take. You're not going to get Julia Roberts thanking me after a take.

QUESTION: How about Rupert? He does a much better job in this film, especially in his handling of the comedy.

    COLUMBUS: I think that Dan and Rupert particularly, and Emma to a certain extent, have become more comfortable. We all knew we weren't going to get fired, so it was a good experience. The first time around, honestly, I got on the set every day and thought I was going to be fired. The kids were terrified because Rupert and Emma had never been on a set before. Rupert couldn't stop looking in the camera the first couple of days of shooting *Sorcerer's Stone*. Suddenly, after 150 days of what was almost this acting workshop, they got confidence, they felt better about themselves, they became accustomed to 250 people on the set. By the time we started shooting the second movie there was a whole level of confidence and ease, and the ability to even do some improvisation, which we had never done before. That all made for a very easy shoot in one sense, time-consuming and intense, energy-wise. By the end of the shoot I couldn't get Rupert to get through a take without smiling or laughing. He was having such a great time. I said to his dad, "Is everything funny to him?" He's amused by everything. His dad said, "He's just very happy. He loves it." So I think that comfort and relaxation shows in the second movie.

QUESTION: Did that sense of relaxation and comfort carry over to the production itself, in the sense that you could flex some more creative freedom and veer from the book a bit?

COLUMBUS: There's certainly a sense out there among kids and among (Potter) fans that *Chamber of Secrets* is not the most popular book. If you ask kids, the first answer you get is *Azkaban*, usually, and that's followed by *Sorcerer's Stone* and *Goblet of Fire*, kind of tied. *Chamber of Secrets* is rarely mentioned. But, from a filmmaking point of view, *Chamber of Secrets* had a hidden little sequence in and of itself, which is that the spider sequence and the basilisk sequence work on the page, from a literary point of view, but they weren't full-blown action sequences. So that's really where we changed a lot. We wanted to develop those into big action sequences.

QUESTION: The first film introduced the world of *Harry Potter* and we got to know all the major characters. This film feels more like characters we know and like are being put on a ride and sent off to have fun. How different a challenge was that for you as the director in that you're not telling as emotional a story?

COLUMBUS: I think it's a combination. I set out to make a film that I knew would be two and a half hours long, but I wanted it to feel like it was about 30 minutes long. I wanted the audience to never be bored, never get tired of it. I was conscious of that. I wanted it to be incredibly exciting for everyone. My main concern was that I wanted to make a film for the parent as well [as the kids], because the parents are there with the kids. And I am sick and tired of sitting in films that I'm bored to death by, that are just aimed directly at kids or below their intelligence level. So that was a conscious effort. From an emotional point of view, I've been knocked around a bunch of times about being too sentimental, so I tried to pull back a little on the emotion. And I realized as I pulled back some of the emotion it became stronger, in a sense. You learn as you get older that by having a little less emotion on screen it becomes a bit of a more emotional experience. So I think it does get emotional, but in a different way.

December 2002

J.K. Rowling made a substantial donation to a Scottish university in their efforts to combat multiple sclerosis. "I became patron of the MS Society Scotland in early 2001," she explained, "after I discovered the appallingly poor quality of care available to people with MS in Scotland, the MS capital of the world. Since then I've been heartened by the huge strides the MS Society Scotland is making, but there is still so much to do, especially in the field of research."

The Leaky Cauldron Web site (www.the-leaky-cauldron.org) turned to its enormous readership to help raise the necessary funds to bid on a 93-word teaser written by J.K. Rowling that provided clues for the next novel, *Order of the Phoenix*. The site's Melissa Anelli explained the site's intentions saying, "We were worried that a wealthy fan would win it and keep its contents private from the millions of fans eagerly waiting for more than two and a half years to find out about the next book."

Warner Brothers asked for permission to shoot portions of *Harry Potter and the Prisoner of Azkaban* at Glencoe in Scotland. Their intention was to make a gatehouse, stone cottages and a sundial garden.

Russian prosecutors claimed they were going to launch an investigation into whether or not the Harry Potter novels served as an instigator of religious hatred. One could ask who exactly those prosecutors would sue.

J.K. Rowling exchanged emails and made phone contact with a young girl named Catie Hoch (to whom Rowling even read over the phone) who was dying of cancer. After the girl's passing, word reached Rowling, and so she wrote to Catie's parents. As reprinted in the *Albany Times Union*, that letter read, in part, "I consider myself privileged to have had contact with Catie. I can only aspire to being the sort of parents both of you have been to Catie during her illness. I am crying so hard as I type. She left footprints on my heart all right. With much love, Jo." Eventually the author donated $100,000 to a charity set up in Catie's name.

The majestic stairway in Christ Church College at Oxford served as the Hogwarts entranceway in the first two films. (Fionna Boyle)

January 2003

In a headline that read "Harry Potter, Get Ready to Meet Count Dracula," MTV reported that Gary Oldman had been offered the role of Sirius Black in *Prisoner of Azkaban*. Noted the actor's manager, Douglas Urbanski, "They've asked him to do *Harry Potter* and I know he's really seriously looking at it. He's delighted to have been offered the role, especially because he's got kids — he's a full-time single dad."

It was revealed that students from the King's School, located next to the Gloucester Cathedral, which stands in for portions of Hogwarts in the Harry Potter films, worked on *The Chamber of Secrets* as extras.

Warner Brothers announced a two-disc DVD release of *Chamber of Secrets* that would hit the streets on April 11.

New York police officers nabbed over 400,000 Ecstasy pills being pushed on the streets that featured an image of Harry Potter on them.

David Thewlis was announced for the role of Professor Lupin in *Prisoner of Azkaban*.

A short surge of controversy as the media began to report that Dobby seemed to feature a too-close-for-comfort resemblance to Vladimir Putin, the president of Russia. Some believed that the filmmakers were mocking Putin.

Fourteen-year-old British citizen Matthew Lawson raised about $5,000 for his education by offering his signed first edition of *The Chamber of Secrets* at auction. Said the teenager, "I am a great fan of J.K. Rowling and Harry Potter and I am sure he would approve of me selling the book to pay for my education. After all, he was lucky enough to go to Hogwarts School of Witchcraft and Wizardry."

Due to her pregnancy, J.K. Rowling served Bloomsbury notice that she would *not* be repeating the massive publicity tour she undertook for the release of *The Goblet of Fire*. In truth, this wasn't deemed a major problem as the books were considered to be strong enough to generate sales on their own.

February 2003

Father Peter Fleetwood, a representative of the Vatican, expressed appreciation for the Harry Potter novels because they helped children see the difference between good and evil. He said, "I don't think there's anyone in this room who grew up without fairies, magic and angels in their imaginary world."

The initial print run of *Harry Potter and the Order of the Phoenix* — to be published on June 21 — was announced to be 6.8 million.

British actor Michael Gambon was announced as the successor of the late Richard Harris in the role of Professor Albus Dumbledore.

Fox announced that J.K. Rowling would be making an animated appearance on an episode of *The Simpsons*. Executive producer Don Payne explained, "The Simpsons bump into J.K. Rowling outside a bookshop and they talk all about Harry Potter. We're very excited about the episode; and rest assured, every British cliché will be trotted out to get a laugh."

March 2003

Both director Alfonso Cuaron and director-turned-producer Chris Columbus discussed with the media the first week of production of

Prisoner of Azkaban. Said Cuaron, "I look forward to bringing this intricate story to the screen and sharing it with film audiences around the world. To be entrusted with such rich and beloved material, and given the opportunity to collaborate with this extraordinary cast and crew on the next Harry Potter adventure is an honor." Added Columbus, "I look forward to seeing it grow as Alfonso and the cast and crew further our imaginations with their truly inspired work. I'm so proud to have been involved in this truly amazing film series, both as a director and a producer."

The ever-vigilant lawyers working for J.K. Rowling turned their sights on a Russian novel titled *Tanya Grotter and The Magic Double Bass*, written by Dimitri Yemetz, which focuses on the magical adventures of a young Russian girl. Noted Rowling's lawyers, "There are three grounds: Copyright infringement, trademark infringement and unfair competition. It copies story line, plot and the characters." Yemetz's Dutch publisher, Byblos, responded, "Tanya Grotter doesn't harm Harry Potter in any way, rather she is his burlesque sister. Yemetz writes his novels both as a parody to the English hero Harry Potter and as a cultural response to the world hype about the mega-bestseller." In the end, the courts found that Tanya Grotter was more than just a parody of Harry, and the publishers were ordered not to allow the novel to be made available to the public.

The Oxford Dictionary said that the word "muggle" would be added to its text. The definition reads: "Muggle (noun) In the fiction of J.K. Rowling, a person who possesses no magical powers. Hence in allusive and extended uses, a person who lacks a particular skill or skills, or who is regarded as inferior in some way."

J.K. Rowling and her husband, Dr. Neil Murray, announced the birth of their son, David Gordon Rowling Murray.

April 2003

While *Prisoner of Azkaban* was being filmed, preparations were already underway for the fourth film, *Harry Potter and The Goblet of Fire*, and for a time it seemed possible that the story would be split into two films rather than one. "We started work on the script last Monday," producer David Heyman said early in the month. "We're going to shoot it as one and see how it ends up. If it's too long, then we'll make it into two." In the end, of course, it would remain one film.

Comedian Dawn French, who spoofed the Harry Potter films during the Comic Relief telecast, found herself cast in the role of the Fat Lady in *Prisoner of Azkaban*. Said producer Chris Columbus, "Yes, Dawn French is portraying the Fat Lady. I think she's incredibly funny and her Harry Potter spoof for Comic Relief was pretty amazing."

An Arkansas judge ordered a ban on Harry Potter books to be lifted, dismissing the notion that the novels encouraged witchcraft.

May 2003

J.K. Rowling announced that she would appear in front of 4,000 children for a reading of part of *Order of the Phoenix* on June 26.

She said that she would also be taking questions from the audience, and would be interviewed on stage by Stephen Fry, who narrates the *Harry Potter* audio editions. The event, it was later reported, would be broadcast on the Internet as well.

When two copies of the yet-to-be-published *Order of the Phoenix* were found in a field near the printing plant, police were called in to investigate. Shortly thereafter, a pair of 16-year-old boys, an 18-year-old boy and a 44-year-old man were arrested and questioned. Rowling's lawyers went into action to get a court-ordered sanction against any of the novel's plot secrets being revealed.

June 2003

Among the things J.K. Rowling discussed with the BBC was her feeling about writing the death of a major character in *Order of the Phoenix* — ultimately revealed to be Sirius Black. "I had rewritten the death, rewritten it and that was it," she said. "It was definitive. And the person was definitely dead. And I walked into the kitchen crying and Neil said to me, 'What on earth is wrong?' and I said, 'Well, I've just killed the person.' Neil doesn't know who the person is. And he said, 'Well, don't do it then.' I thought, 'Well, it just doesn't work like that. You are writing children's books, you need to be a ruthless killer.'"

The *Washington Post* featured a story on the explosion of fan fiction on the Internet. "Fan fiction has existed for decades," noted the story, "but primarily as a fringe hobby among friends who passed along typed or handwritten manuscripts to one another.

But thanks to the ubiquity of the Internet, it has jumped into the popular consciousness with a following so large that it is now a topic of graduate theses and [the focus of] writing contests and a significant marketing outlet for media corporations. One of the largest collections of fan fiction is built on Harry Potter. On FanFiction.net alone, the granddaddy of fan-fiction sites, there are some 75,000 stories about the character."

The *New York Daily News* found itself in deep trouble when they apparently received early information on *Order of the Phoenix* and went public with a number of tidbits. Rumors of lawsuits from Rowling and her publishers began flying, though apparently nothing ever came of them. Spokesman Ken Frydman said, "We will vigorously defend any action and are confident we did nothing wrong journalistically or legally."

The CBS *Early Show* offered a story on the growing anticipation for *Order of the Phoenix* and the sales records broken in bookstores, both traditional and online. Amazon's Bill Carr noted, "We have more than 660,000 preorders we've taken for *Harry Potter and the Order of the Phoenix* in the U.S. and more than one million world-wide."

Zap2it.com reported that props were stolen from the Glencoe, Scotland, location for *Prisoner of Azkaban*.

J.K. Rowling was interviewed by the BBC, where she admitted that she had begun to feel a bit guilty about the wealth she had accumulated thanks to Harry Potter. "The biggest jump for me," she said, "was the American advance which was enough for me to buy a house, not outright, but you know we'd been renting until then. And I didn't feel guilty, I felt scared at that point. Because I thought I mustn't blow this; I've got some money, I mustn't do anything stupid with it. And then, yeah, I felt guilty. I mean, at least I could see cause and effect. I knew I had worked quite hard for quite a long time."

Theage.com offered an in-depth look at the popularity of Harry Potter in an article called "Why Harry Potter is So Magical." In that piece they note, "Rowling's signal achievement has been to take the traditional boarding school story and to link it with a world of magic, with a universe that is full of deep wells of good and evil activated at the touch of a wand in the hand of a master wizard. . . . It's a wonderful world, the world of Hogwarts, because it is deeply rooted in the world we know, of eccentric schoolteachers and kids (even nice kids) being cruel to each other. But then there is the magic — that's why everyone's here — and it summons up a world of dragons and giant spiders and every kind of horror and threat. . . . Rowling has created the highest level of bestseller popular fiction: a series of books that are going to entertain and enchant young people as well as their grandparents. She has written a set of stories that people will be reading for a long time yet and that will continue to be made into films and television shows the way Sherlock Holmes is or Agatha Christie or Superman."

To give a sense of the type of mania surrounding the publication of *Order of the Phoenix*, *USA Today* provided a report regarding an Arlington, Virginia, Barnes & Noble: "Store staff passed out numbered orange wristbands to customers who had preordered copies and red raffle tickets to those who had not — and Harry glasses to all. Customers began arriving around 7 p.m. to pick up raffle tickets. By 11 p.m. there were about 300 people crowding the store, and staff had given out the last tickets for unreserved books. . . . Shortly before 11:30 p.m., staff began calling customers by wristband and ticket numbers to begin forming lines, just like airline personnel call passengers to board a plane. . . . Following a countdown to 12:01 a.m., the books were unveiled to cheering and applause. . . . The store sold its last copies within 40 minutes of opening on Saturday."

A self-proclaimed witch named Marysia Kolodziel, who resides in London, offered this view of Harry Potter: "I am a fan for several reasons. Initially it's the universe, the books with the largest pull have this highly detailed, well-thought-out universe that almost seems real and, importantly, that you would want to be a part of. You are not just drawn into the story but into that world. Then, through talking about them with fans, you fall further and further in love with the characters, you analyze them and worry about them until they feel real to you. Then you have, in a way, become a part of that shared universe and it is a wonderful place to be."

A Kansas City postal worker named Kenia Cooper was reportedly almost fired for delivering a single copy of *Order of the Phoenix* one day too early as part of her regular duties despite its being marked for delivery no earlier than June 21. Rightly she pointed out, "I'm paid to do a job, I did a job. It's a book — it's fiction — and this is my real life. This is not fiction. Me having to fight for my job is not fiction." Shortly after this story hit the media, the post office claimed she was only suspended, not fired.

Reading an excerpt from the new novel in front of 4,000 children at Royal Albert Hall in England, J.K. Rowling reflected, "The first reading I did was to two people who had wandered into the basement of Waterstone's by mistake, and were too polite to walk out because somebody was doing a reading." She added that if she could have one power a day, she would choose invisibility so that she could continue doing what she used to do — write her novels while sitting in cafes.

Bloomsbury threatened legal action against Internet pirates who attempted to post a scanned copy of *Order of the Phoenix* on the Internet.

J.K. Rowling signs a copy of Order of the Phoenix *for a young wizard in Edinburgh. (Jeff J. Mitchell/Reuters/Corbis)*

July 2003

Maranatha Christian College, located in Australia, banned the Harry Potter novels because they put the idea of wizardry, something the college deemed evil, in a positive light. Principal Bart Langerak said, "As Christians, witchcraft and the occult are considered evil. It has been widely publicized that many children have tried to cast spells as a result of reading the books, and that is not a view we want held. We would deal with, say, *Macbeth* and *Hamlet*, because evil there is being portrayed as evil, and not as being good."

Getting permission from Warner Brothers and J.K. Rowling, dancers from Derbyshire and Staffordshire took part in a ballet based on *Harry Potter and the Chamber of Secrets*. Mrs. Parrott (no first name given) from the troupe explained, "The music is beautifully composed by John Williams, and the fast movements in the Quidditch scenes and the elf-like movement of Dobby — we just went from there. I went to watch the *Chamber of Secrets* film and in one scene Harry's rival Draco says, 'So you are training for the ballet, Potter?' and I thought, 'I can do a ballet!'"

The house used for the Dursleys' place of residence in the first film in the series was put up for sale at a price of nearly half a million dollars.

More legal Harry Potter problems: This time in the form of Chinese fans who illegally posted translated copies of *Order of the Phoenix* online. Also more Web problems domestically as the novel became available as illegal e-books. A lawyer at J.K. Rowling's literary agency, Neil Blair, said, "E-book rights are reserved to J.K. Rowling. So any Harry Potter novels on the Net are unauthorized. We also have an obligation to protect the children who might believe they are reading the official work."

Thanks largely to the success of *Order of the Phoenix*, Amazon.com saw its profits raised by 37 percent.

August 2003

While *Prisoner of Azkaban* was still shooting, word surfaced that the producers of the Harry Potter films were talking to Mike Newell (*Four Weddings and a Funeral*, *Donnie Brasco*) about helming film number four, *Goblet of Fire*. This eventually turned out to be true, with Newell exclaiming, "I'm very excited about directing *Harry Potter and the Goblet of Fire*. As audiences have become more familiar with both the books and the movies, there has been an increasing challenge to continue to develop each of these characters and to make their world real on screen." Calling Newell the perfect choice, producer David Heyman added, "He has worked with children, made us laugh and had us sitting on the edge of our seats. He is great with actors, and imbues all his characters, all his films, with great humanity. I'm thrilled." The film was scheduled to start shooting in April 2004.

The efforts of author and artist James Downey to get J.K. Rowling considered for a Nobel Prize didn't seem to have any impact on those making such decisions. As to his reasons for doing so, and his efforts to use the Internet to galvanize fans, Downey said, "Uniting millions of people around the globe to attempt this ostensibly impossible task is a new kind of performance art."

September 2003

The train used as the Hogwarts Express was vandalized with graffiti. The cost of removing it was estimated to be $5,000.

The late Richard Harris's sons, Damian, Jared and Jamie, held a memorial tribute to their father at a London theater. Among the 300 people attending were Alan Rickman, who plays Professor Snape; and Richard Griffiths, who plays Harry's uncle, Vernon Dursley.

October 2003

Emma Thompson joined the cast of *Prisoner of Azkaban* as Professor Trelawney, the Divinations instructor. Interestingly, Thompson's ex-husband, Kenneth Branagh, had been cast as Defense Against the Dark Arts professor Gilderoy Lockhart in *Chamber of Secrets*.

Working with the producers of the Harry Potter films, J.K. Rowling arranged for two cameo roles in *Prisoner of Azkaban* to be awarded to the highest bidders in a charity auction for MS. "Being able to campaign for multiple sclerosis is the most meaningful thing to have come out of being famous," said Rowling. "It would mean everything to me if I thought even one person did not have to go through what my mother did."

In an interview with the BBC, Daniel Radcliffe confirmed that he would be returning in the role of Harry in *Goblet of Fire*. One of the reasons, he said, is that, "It always feels good working with Emma, Rupert, Tom [Felton, who plays Draco] and Matthew [Lewis, who plays Neville]. We have become very good friends and as this is now the third film we have made together our relationships just get stronger."

J.K. Rowling traveled to Spain to receive the Prince of Asturias Award for Concord for her contribution to the arts, and for the "moral" aspects of her novels. Said Rowling, "I certainly didn't set out to teach, or to preach, to children. I wanted to depict the ambiguities of a society where bigotry, cruelty, hypocrisy and corruption are rife, the better to show how truly heroic it is, whatever your age, to fight a battle that can never be won. And I also wanted to reflect the fact that life can be difficult and confusing between the ages of 11 and 17, even when armed with a wand."

At the end of the month it was announced that a 90-second teaser trailer for *Prisoner of Azkaban* would be attached to Warner Brothers' *Looney Tunes: Back in Action*.

In an interview appearing on the *Azkaban* Web site, Daniel Radcliffe compared the experience of working with directors Chris Columbus and Alfonso Cuaron. "First of all," he said, "I consider myself very lucky to have worked with two great directors on these films. Chris is without a doubt the most energetic director I have ever met. He was amazing in keeping us motivated and in encouraging us every step of the way. Alfonso, on the other hand, directs in a more intense way. The scenes in this film are some of the most passionate and emotional I have ever worked on, and Alfonso's style has been very helpful to me."

According to *Scotland on Sunday*, J.K. Rowling pulled in over $200 million in royalties during 2003.

November 2003

Offering a first glimpse of *Prisoner*, *USA Today* reported, "Werewolves and dementors are one thing, but how about teen hormones for something really scary? . . . This movie, which arrives in theaters June 4, 2004, is spookier, darker and more emotional, with a more adolescent and angry Harry Potter, now 13, a new

Professor Dumbledore and a more contemporary look for Harry and his pals, Ron and Hermione. All of this from a new director, Alfonso Cuaron. 'Alfonso really understands the nuances of being a teenager, and that's vital to this film,' producer David Heyman says. 'It's much more grounded in reality. This is a magical world, but not a fantasy world.'"

Welsh comic Paul Whitehouse was added to the cast of *Azkaban* as Sir Cadogan, a knight who becomes the temporary guardian of Gryffindor Tower.

MGM announced a spoof of both Harry Potter and *Lord of the Rings* in the form of something called *Henry Bates and the Sorcerer's Balls*. Thankfully this one hasn't been made. Yet.

According to the BBC, sales of the first five Harry Potter novels reached an incredible 250 million copies. J.K. Rowling's agent, Christopher Little, noted, "J.K. Rowling's books have paved the way for a new generation of exciting children's writers, causing a revolution in children's enthusiasm for reading."

J.K. Rowling's father, Peter, desperate to raise cash and too proud to ask his daughter for help, put five first editions on the auction block, each of those books personally inscribed by his daughter. According to one report he was hoping to raise $200,000.

Toward the end of the month, filming wrapped on *Prisoner of Azkaban*, and Warner Brothers celebrated the event with a major party. Reported the Web site HPANA (Harry Potter Automatic News Aggregator), "Warner Brothers had, without a doubt, put on a fantastic show. There was a huge bonfire leading up to the main area, the marquees were massive with two Knight Buses lit up brilliantly with different colored lights, a stage in the middle (mainly being used by an absolutely awesome Mexican band)."

Moscow fans clamor for a copy of the Russian edition of Order of the Phoenix, *released in February 2004. (Sergei Karpukhin/Reuters/Corbis)*

The Web site www.int.iol.co.za presented an article called "Harry Potter Game is Enchanting Youngsters," which told of a gym teacher named Justin van Gelder who decided to incorporate the game Quidditch into his curriculum. "The kids don't fly and we have control of the balls," he explained. According to the article, in Van Gelder's class a pair of hula hoops are propped upright between folded mats on either side of the gymnasium. Determined third graders with foam balls in hand try to avoid being tagged out by the "bludgers" — students holding yarn balls — before they can score. Every few minutes, the instructor, using a rubber ball as a stand-in for a "golden snitch," throws one into the game. Two "seekers" try to grab the ball and earn their team 150 points. When the snitch is not in play, the "seekers" are responsible for freeing any teammates who have been tagged out by the "bludgers." Added Van Gelder, "The great thing about the whole Harry Potter aspect is that the kids are so into it. They pay attention and really want to learn the right way to play the game."

Harry Potter and the Chamber of Secrets was named most popular film in the British Academy Children's Film and Television Awards. Among the celebrities in attendance at the awards was Hermione Granger herself, Emma Watson.

December 2003

Both Gary Oldman and Jason Isaacs spoke to *Empire* magazine about their respective roles of Sirius Black and Lucius Malfoy. Said Oldman, "Alfonso has his own take on it. I think it's going to be the best one yet, but I *would* say that." Isaacs added, "Just as we were finishing *Chamber of Secrets*, Alfonso Cuaron came along and I got to shake hands with him and that was about it. I don't know what's happening with *Goblet of Fire*; I don't know whether they're going to put Lucius Malfoy in or not. If I thought begging would do any good, I'd be out there every day. But that would probably just irritate them."

While speaking to Sci Fi Wire, *Goblet of Fire* director Mike Newell said that he intended to pick up where Alfonso Cuaron left off. "What Alfonso has done very remarkably is he's developed the films from a sunny vision of childhood into something that is much darker and blacker," he said. "And he's done that without taking away any of the romance of the thing. But he has transformed it into adolescence, and I must go on from what he's done. I can't go back."

Shefali Chowdhury and Ashan Azad won the coveted roles of Parvati and Padma Patil in Goblet of Fire. *(INFGoff.com/CP Photo)*

The BBC noted that the producers of the Harry Potter films were looking for twin girls to play Parvati and Padma. The auditions were to be held at the Pineapple Studios in London. Said casting director Shaheen Baig, "In this book [*Goblet of Fire*] they are actually written as twins, but it has been incredibly difficult to find Asian twin girls, so we decided to open it up and just find two girls. We're looking for two girls — if they happen to be sisters, that would be amazing, but it doesn't really matter. We just want two good girls who have fantastic chemistry."

IMAX struck a deal to release a giant-screen version of *Harry Potter and the Prisoner of Azkaban* to IMAX theaters in June 2004.

Warner Brothers lost its legal bid to shut down a "Harry Potter" clothing line developed and sold by the Australian chain Wombat — mainly because the line came into existence several years prior to J.K. Rowling creating Harry Potter. Wombat co-owner Clair Jennifer commented, "This is a definite story of a huge multi-national trying to squash what they thought was a small business in Australia. What they didn't understand was our actual size — we are national and very well-known in our industry." Justice Murray Wilcox said in his ruling, "Although it may be accepted that a person who first hears the name Harry Potter today would most likely think of the J.K. Rowling character, it seems to me unlikely that a person seeing the 'Harry Potter' label on clothing in a Wombat boutique would assume a connection."

A signed first edition of *Harry Potter and the Goblet of Fire* fetched about $40,000 at an auction held at Sotheby's.

The BBC reported, "About 2,000 Asian teenagers have queued around London's West End for a chance to star in the next Harry Potter film. Girls braved the cold on Sunday to take part in an open audition for the parts of twins Parvati and Padma in *Harry Potter and the Goblet of Fire*. They came from as far as Liverpool and Cardiff to the Pineapple Studios in Langley Street, near Covent Garden. But they did not get a chance to show off their acting talents, as producers just wanted to photograph each girl. They said acting experience was not as important as getting the right look for the twins, who accompany Harry and Ron to the school ball in the book."

January 2004

Strange rumors were afoot that British funny man Rowan Atkinson was going to be cast as Voldemort in *Goblet of Fire*, but these turned out to be false. As Atkinson's agent, Janette Linden, explained to the BBC, "There's no truth whatsoever that Rowan will be in the next Harry Potter movie."

Harry Potter and the Order of the Phoenix was nominated in the category of Best Fiction at the WH Smith Book Awards.

Emma Watson confirmed that she would be returning as Hermione in *Goblet of Fire*. "I will be doing film four," she said. "As for the future, just going with the flow, see what happens."

While talking to the *San Bernardino County Sun*, producer David Heyman said of Harry in *Prisoner of Azkaban*, "Harry has a bit more of the attitude of a 13-year-old. He's growing up and, I think, the films are growing up. This third one is a little edgier, a little darker. It's funny, it's charming, it still has a lot of the qualities of the first two films, but it is also dealing with different external fears." Added Alfonso Cuaron, who tried to draw comparisons between this and his previous film, *Y Tu Mamá También*, "The themes are very similar. *Y Tu Mamá También* is about teenagers seeking their adult identities, and *Azkaban* is about children looking for their identities as teenagers. I think that Harry Potter films can be very, very fun rides, but there are a lot of other readings to the materials, so this theme could come through."

Amusingly, Queen Elizabeth of England proved to a group of children that she had a better working knowledge of the Harry Potter universe than even they did, answering trivia questions that they couldn't. Now *that's* impressive.

Amazing what will sell at an auction: An uncorrected proof copy of the first Harry Potter novel, with J.K. Rowling's name spelled wrong, was sold for nearly $2,000.

When the budget to *Goblet of Fire* was rumored to be north of $130 million, director Mike Newell noted, "These things are not like ordinary films. They are world events. I have millions of 10-year-olds who must not be disappointed. Making *Harry Potter* is like being president of Brazil. It is a colossal undertaking."

According to *Hello!* magazine, J.K. Rowling was voted the most powerful woman in Hollywood.

In casting the role of Cho Chang in *Goblet of Fire*, the producers were reportedly very specific about what they were looking for. "Would-be Chos must be of Southeast Asian appearance," stated the BBC, "look around 16 years old and must live in the UK. Girls who don't match up won't be able to apply. . . . The girl who plays Cho will have a brilliant role. She's the Hogwarts pupil on whom Harry gets a crush."

February 2004

The *Los Angeles Times* published a story on *Prisoner of Azkaban* that featured a number of interesting comments from those involved with its production. Said Alan Horn, President of Warner Brothers, "Y *Tu Mamá También* confirmed to me that Alfonso could live in the world of fantasy and children and not be treacly, and also be a little bit dark. And he got such performances out of those two young boys. Now our protagonists in *Harry Potter* are 13, entering puberty, and he understands that. The question was: Could he handle something of this size? It can be daunting." For his part, Cuaron admitted, "I have to confess, I was a bit ignorant about the Harry Potter thing. So I read Steve Kloves' script, and it was great. And then I immediately read the book. And I was, frankly, amazed by the book and the script. . . . Harry goes through a journey where he realizes that demons aren't just things that go bump in the night, but also can be painful emotions, worries about family, friends, the future, the monsters that lie within. And that's a classic teenage issue. . . . The whole goal of taking a franchise in a new direction is what keeps [it] alive. Jo Rowling said to me, 'Don't be literal. Just be faithful to the spirit.' You might have hits and misses, but it's always going to be fresh." Director-turned-producer Chris Columbus emphasized one point: "I wanted to make sure that the film didn't stray too far from the world that the audience and the fans have sort of fallen in love with over the course of the first two movies."

Although details were scarce, it was reported that the UK optical firm Graham Coates had begun working on effects for *Goblet of Fire*.

In an interview with *Empire* magazine, director Mike Newell addressed the rumors that *Goblet of Fire* might be split into two films. "As far as I'm concerned," he said, "it's absolutely possible to do it in one. I think it would be slightly embarrassing to do it in two. It's a classic paranoid thriller in a way. I've spent Christmas watching things like *The Parallax View* and *The Insider* and *Three*

Days of the Condor. What you have is a story at the beginning of which the powers of evil have a plan, which is absolutely not revealed to your hero. The kid just wanders into another year at school, then this huge notion of the competition surprises him. But there is, of course, a malign interference which is manipulating things. And so he gets more and more suspicious until there is a shoot-out between him and the bad guy. That's a really good, strong thriller shape."

The French magazine *Studio* reported (incorrectly, it turned out) that actress Carole Bouquet (the wife of Gérard Depardieu and, incidentally, the leading Bond lady in 1981's *For Your Eyes Only*) had been cast in *Goblet of Fire*.

The *Times* Educational Supplement reported that hundreds of Bulgarian teenage boys decided to cut from school in order to audition for the part of Victor Krum in *Harry Potter and the Goblet of Fire*.

John Hurt announced he would be returning as Mr. Ollivander in *Goblet*, though the actor nearly said no to the offer. "I was going to turn it down," said Hurt, "but I was told by my girlfriend and my agent that if I didn't do it, my children would never speak to me." This, of course, mirrored the comment made to the late Richard Harris by his granddaughter, which "guilted" him into the role of Dumbledore.

In an interview with *Empire* magazine, Emma Thompson discussed her *Prisoner of Azkaban* character, Professor Trelawney. "I decided that since she was someone who saw into the future, she had to be someone who couldn't see anything at all in the present," she said. "Like where she was going, her clothing. . . . anything. I decided to dress her slightly differently, and had wonderful cooperation from my director and designer and everything."

A statue of Harry Potter built of Lego on display at the Toys R Us store in Times Square, New York. (Fionna Boyle)

Lego announced six new sets based on *The Prisoner of Azkaban*.

J.K. Rowling's personal fortune continued to rise, with one estimate being approximately $1 billion. To celebrate, she participated at a charity auction, spending more than £125,000.

March 2004

Could there be future adventures of Harry Potter beyond the seven books J.K. Rowling swore the character would be limited to? In a Web chat she noted, "I'll never say never, because every time I do, I immediately break the vow." Needless to say, this sparked worldwide media attention.

J.K. Rowling was among those invited to a "girl power" lunch held by the Queen of England. At about the same time, she was awarded the fiction prize at the annual WH Smith People's Choice Book Awards for *Harry Potter and the Order of the Phoenix*. Said Rowling of her longest book to date, "This is wonderful. Unabashed adult Harry Potter fans are very dear to my heart, and obviously in the case of *The Order of the Phoenix* they were the ones who were physically able to lift the book."

In a *USA Today* article on *Prisoner of Azkaban*, Alfonso Cuaron discussed the fact that he had his young cast write essays about their characters. "The kids were very brave," he said. "They bared their souls. They were very eloquent. At some point, I wanted to publish them, then I thought, 'No.' I promised them it was just for the work of the film and it's their personal stuff. We had free-flowing discussions about what it means to be 13. How it's different from 12 or 11. It's an archetypal age. Kids change so much. You want to change the way you dress, the way you look, the way you argue."

Second-unit filming on *Goblet of Fire* got underway toward the end of the month in Scotland.

A loan of about $7,000 from a friend had allowed J.K. Rowling, who was suffering from severe fiscal difficulties, to finish writing the first Harry Potter novel. Said Rowling, "I broke down and cried when my friend offered it to me. At the time it was like half a million pounds to me. It was this enormous sum of money. I think we both thought I would never be able to pay it back. The friend was saying in effect, 'Here is a gift to help you.'" In return, and once Rowling's creation turned out to be such a phenomenon, she reportedly repaid this friend by buying her a house that is currently worth about $400,000.

A teenager from Chile traveled to London, tricked into believing she had been invited there by Daniel Radcliffe. When she showed up at the Radcliffe residence with emails purportedly written by Daniel in hand, the young actor's father, Alan, had the sad duty of telling her she had been duped. Said Alan Radcliffe, "Daniel never communicates with fans via the Internet or email for this very reason — he doesn't want anyone to be duped into corresponding with someone pretending to be him. For his fans' sake and safety there are no exceptions to this rule, and anyone claiming to be Daniel Radcliffe is, I'm afraid, lying."

A rumor arose that *Titanic*'s Kate Winslet had been offered the role of a wizard in *Goblet of Fire*, but this turned out to be false.

An unofficial Harry Potter convention was announced for October 6–11, 2005, to be held in Salem, Massachusetts, under the name "The Witching Hour: A Harry Potter Symposium." Said coordinator Melissa Lee, "Halloween is such a huge aspect to the Harry Potter books. The best place to have the conference is in Salem, America's backyard at Halloween time."

One report has it that Daniel Radcliffe's personal fortune after the release of the first two Harry Potter films was about $9 million.

April 2004

The ABC network announced that when it aired *Harry Potter and the Sorcerer's Stone* on May 9, it would include a 10-minute preview of *Prisoner of Azkaban*.

Due to the vast territory covered in *Goblet of Fire*, all sequences from the novel featuring the Dursleys had been dropped from the film. Richard Griffiths, who played Vernon Dursley in the first three films, says that he approached J.K. Rowling about the situation. Said Griffiths, "I asked, 'Couldn't the Dursleys show up to an Open Day at Harry's school or something?' But she said, 'I don't think so.'"

Warner Brothers announced that *Goblet of Fire* would be released on November 18, 2005.

Time magazine announced that as far as they were concerned, J.K. Rowling had become one of the top 100 most influential people in the world.

Comingsoon.com reported that Warner Brothers had launched an all-new Web experience devoted to *Prisoner of Azkaban*. "In addition to serving as a comprehensive promotional site dedicated to the magical world of Harry Potter," they posted, "the newly unveiled site features exclusive interactive content and news about the third installment of the blockbuster film series."

Humorously, Daniel Radcliffe stated he can't watch *Sorcerer's Stone* because of the sound of his own voice. "Actually," he said, "I was flicking through the channels one day and I saw a bit of the first film and I genuinely thought there was something wrong with it. It sounded like I was on helium, it was bizarre." Elsewhere he commented on the essay he had to write for Alfonso Cuaron on his character. "It was really funny," he said, "because the way we did it was exactly how our characters would do it. I did it like Harry, just a page of writing. Rupert didn't do it in the end and Emma wrote sixteen pages. So we were like, 'Oh, God, we've all become scarily like our characters.'"

Fox 23 reported that John Malkovich had been signed to play Voldemort in *Goblet of Fire*, and even quoted an anonymous source, "He is perfect for the role. He will play the 'restored' human version of Lord Voldemort and has a spectacular fight with Harry at the end of the film." In the end, they got the fight part right, though they were wrong about the actor.

Jason Isaacs confirmed that he would be returning as Lucius Malfoy. In an interview with *The Sun* he stated, "I make a tiny cameo appearance in the fourth film, to remind people that I still exist as I have a bit more to do in the fifth one. To be honest, I thought I wouldn't get to be in the fourth film at all, but it will be nice to get the wig out of mothballs and start the slow warm-up for number five where I have some rather juicy and lovely stuff."

Apparently J.K. Rowling was asked to write an episode of the BBC sci-fi series *Doctor Who*, but she had to turn down the request due to schedule conflicts.

The *Daily Record* revealed that 16-year-old Katie Leung had been cast as Cho Chang in *Goblet of Fire*. Said her father, Peter, "It's obviously a great part to get, and it's a happy time for all the family. Katie is supposed to be getting a press officer and things like that." That publication also featured an interview with Daniel Radcliffe, in which he discussed part of the downside of fame. "When the first two films came out," he said, "I had to have bodyguards because I created such a ruckus everywhere I went. That was absolutely no fun. I really pray *The Prisoner of Azkaban* doesn't make me really famous again, because I love being completely anonymous and I've felt like that for almost two years. When I'm on the streets of a big city like New York and no one recognizes me, it reminds me that I'm just a normal teenager. And that's all I am. Don't get me wrong. I love the fact that I was given the chance to portray Harry Potter. Even J.K. Rowling thanked me for playing the role."

May 2004

While speaking to the *Washington Post*, Alfonso Cuaron discussed, among other things, how obligated he was to stick to the novel of *Prisoner of Azkaban*. Said the director, "I was very happy that very early on I had great advice from J.K. Rowling: 'Be faithful to the spirit of the book, don't be literal.' There are a lot of things we lose because we do not have the time. So we decide to stick to this theme of this rite of passage. Whatever sticks into that theme we keep it in, and leave out whatever does not." In the pages of *Premiere* magazine, screenwriter Steve Kloves addressed the same issue of what to keep and what to cut. "Kids have often said we cut too many things out; adults think they're way too long," he explained. "So we find ourselves in this weird place. I made some big cuts in *Harry Potter and the Prisoner of Azkaban*. Alfonso wanted to talk about the inner terrain of the characters, and we addressed each scene with the idea of their taking a step into adolescence. It may only be a couple of years' difference, but it's an absolute Grand Canyon in terms of the emotional distance. . . . Jo is tremendously supportive and she understands the differences between the books and the movies."

Daniel Radcliffe was stunned by the sheer fervor of the fans who greeted him and others at the New York premiere of *Prisoner of Azkaban*. Enthused Radcliffe, "It's astonishing — it's really, really, really scary, but it's brilliant. We have worked on the film for 11 months and it's really gratifying that everyone came out to support it. It's amazing. And they should support it, because it's a great film."

Brendan Gleeson, whose credits include *Gangs of New York*, *Cold Mountain* and *The Village*, joined the cast of *Goblet of Fire* as Mad-Eye Moody. Also added to the cast was Frances de la Tour as the half-giant Madame Maxine.

In an interview with *The Scotsman*, Gary Oldman explained not only that he was grateful for the work of *Prisoner of Azkaban*, but also that he considered playing Sirius Black something of an honor. "It's prestigious," he said. "You're not just making a movie — it's joining a family of some kind of cinematic dynasty, I suppose. It's interesting to be part of that. The material was good and the director was interesting. I've got three kids who like *Harry Potter*, so it's nice to actually be in a movie that they can see, as opposed to a job that takes me away for twelve hours a day."

J.K. Rowling announced that she was "well under way" on book number six. "I am really enjoying this book," she said, "though for the first time I am conscious that I am approaching the end of the series. So much of what happens in book six relates to book seven that I feel almost as though they are two halves of the same novel."

Alfonso Cuaron expressed to Reuters his hope that the core cast for the Harry Potter films would stay the same for all seven chapters. "Right now they're doing number four," he pointed out. "There's only three more to go. I just hope they keep the same cast for the whole thing. So far, they're holding up very good, the way they are aging. I don't think Dan is going to get way much taller or suddenly grow another eye. Same with Emma, and Rupert is okay. Let's hope. My dream is that the cast would remain intact."

Some interesting musings from Daniel Radcliffe regarding the ultimate fate of Harry Potter. "I'm going to be really unpopular for saying this," he told the BBC, "but I've always had the suspicion that Harry might die. Harry and Voldemort have the same core in them, and the only way he could die is if Harry dies as well." If J.K. Rowling is following patterns of epic fantasy story structure à la King Arthur or *Lord of the Rings*, that could indeed be a possibility.

J.K. Rowling's representatives let it be known that she was flattered by all of the fan fiction that is devoted to her creation. "Her concern," said the spokesperson, "would be to make sure that it remains a non-commercial activity to ensure fans are not exploited and it is not being published in the strict sense of traditional print publishing."

J.K. Rowling updated her Web site (www.jkrowling.com) by including more hints and trivia about the Harry Potter universe.

According to the BBC, Vue Cinemas in Britain came up with a new way to seek out those who illegally videotape films: employees don night-vision goggles. The idea was that anyone caught with a camcorder would be reported to the police.

June 2004

Speaking with AP, Daniel Radcliffe admitted that he was interested in an entertainment career beyond acting: "I'd like to be in a band — a really good band. Guitar music — but like good, intelligent guitar music. Hopefully, I've just got to work hard and prove to people that I can do other things."

Interesting tidbit, according to www.zap2it.com, Ron's rat Scabbers is actually a West African rodent that was imported from a Berlin zoo. Possibly one of the few non-British cast members to appear in a Harry Potter film.

Some people always look for ways to ruin things for others: a computer virus known as the "P worm" was spread disguised as a Harry Potter game.

A survey for the Prince of Wales Arts and Kids Foundation concluded that Harry Potter was more popular among children than such classics as the *Lord of the Rings* trilogy, *The Jungle Book* and *Winnie the Pooh.*

Emma Watson was genuinely scared when a reporter for the British prank series *Ministry of Mayhem* asked her to recreate the moment from *Prisoner of Azkaban* where she punches out Draco Malfoy. What poor Emma didn't suspect is that prankmeister Stephen Mulhern had placed fake blood capsules in his mouth, which made it look like she had done some serious damage to his face. Don't worry, though, it wasn't long before Emma caught on.

Robbie Coltrane admitted that he didn't necessarily enjoy the rigors of Hagrid's makeup and costume. "It's revolting having your face covered in glue," he said. "It's a horrible, horrible, thing and the only downside of these wonderful films for me. It also means that kids never recognize me. They just know Hagrid — and I am buried under tons of makeup, beard and costume."

In an interview with *USA Today*, Gary Oldman commented on the importance of Harry Potter to British pride: "When one thinks of Britain," he said, "it's the royal family, Buckingham Palace, The Rolling Stones, The Beatles, Harry Potter. It's as English as strawberry jam and scones."

French actress Clémence Poésy was announced in the role of Fleur Delacour in *Harry Potter and the Goblet of Fire*.

An interesting article in *USA Today* noted the following: "Despite the movie's dark premise, some experts say the film's overarching theme of confronting and overcoming fears — a common thread through much of the series about the young wizard — sends a positive message to young viewers." In the same article, Bethesda, Maryland, clinical psychologist Syd Brown said, "Superficially, it's about witches and wizards and magic and all that other stuff. In fact, it's a tribute to perseverance and resilience."

Proving itself to be a continuing fount of information on the world of Harry Potter, *USA Today* reviewed the *Prisoner of Azkaban* video game, offering, "The spectacular graphics make the world come alive. Water flows, fabrics billow, and the Hogwarts castle is presented in amazing detail as kids turn the camera 360 degrees to view vaulted ceilings or mosaic floors. The two previous Harry Potter games were great, and this one is even better."

Bloomsbury made no secret of the fact that it was placing a lot of hope on the paperback edition of *Order of the Phoenix*.

Toward the end of the month filming began on *Harry Potter and the Goblet of Fire*.

The Internet went crazy with the rumor that book number six was going to be called *Harry Potter and the Pillar of Storge*. "I nearly fell off my chair giggling when I read that," admitted J.K. Rowling, who announced that the book would actually be called *Harry Potter and the Half-Blood Prince*, an alternate title for book number two, *The Chamber of Secrets*. "Certain crucial pieces of information in book six were originally planned for *Chamber of Secrets*, but very early on I realized that this information's proper home was book six. I have said before now that *Chamber* holds some very important clues to the ultimate end of the series."

Harry Potter and the Prisoner of Azkaban was released on June 4, 2004. It scored an opening weekend gross of $93,687,367. Domestically it went on to gross $249,541,069, its international take was $540,263,485, for a global total of $789,804,554.

As was the case with its predecessors, at the time of *Prisoner of Azkaban*'s release, cast and crew met with the press. What follows are edited transcripts of some of those sessions.

ALFONSO CUARON
(Director)

QUESTION: Were you surprised to get this job?

Alfonso Cuaron at the New York premiere of Prisoner of Azkaban. *(Shannon Stapleton/Reuters/Corbis)*

ALFONSO CUARON: First, I was kind of amused when they proposed the whole thing. I was so ignorant of the Harry Potter universe that I actually received the script and I just put it in a pile.

QUESTION: You didn't even read it?
CUARON: No. But David Heyman who's a fine producer called me and said, "What do you think?" I said, "I don't know." He said, "Please read it, because I really want you to do it, but I really need to give an answer." I read the script and I was like, "Whoa, okay." Then I read the book and after I read the book, I said, "Okay, I have to do this film."

QUESTION: Did you see the first two films?
CUARON: I saw the first two and then I read the rest of the books.

QUESTION: Is this one darker because of what was in the book or because of your style?

> **CUARON:** I think that it was just the subject matter. Harry is growing up. Everything is his perception of the world, and that's becoming darker and more mature, a little more introspective.

QUESTION: At what point did Richard Harris die?

> **CUARON:** Very early into the process Richard Harris passed. That was a big blow for everyone on *Harry Potter*. I mean, the only thing that I can say I was lucky with was that I was the only one who never had the fortune to meet him. He actually was David Heyman's godfather. So that was a very tough one. So we decided for many months to not even mention looking for a new actor. It took many months before we were ready to start looking for actors and talking about names.

QUESTION: How did Michael Gambon's name come up?

> **CUARON:** Michael Gambon is one of the most powerful actors out there. He has such an amazing presence and command. I'm very, very, very grateful for what Michael did in this film.

QUESTION: Aren't there a lot of differences between the book and the movie?

> **CUARON:** Just in terms of the logistics. Because I have to say, in terms of the spirit, I think that it's very, very faithful to the spirit of the book. Now Jo Rowling's said from the get-go, "Be faithful to the spirit. Don't try to be literal." So when you do that, you just have to take certain shortcuts. It was clear that we didn't want to spend time in Diagon Alley this time, just to give you an example. But at the same time, we wanted to start with the *Monster Book of Monsters*. So we had to make a separate scene where we established the book that is in Harry's bedroom. It's stuff like that. It's about finding short-cuts or ways to convey the information cinematically.

QUESTION: Was it difficult finding a look for the dementors?

CUARON: First of all, in terms of the design with the dementors, the thing is that you have the most amazing iconography of black hooded creatures in cinema. Not only in cinema, but in art. But then Peter Jackson did the ultimate black hooded character [in *Lord of the Rings*], and we were saying, "Well, what are we going to do? He did it so beautifully," and it wasn't until one of my many revisits to *Lord of the Rings* — I was watching the first one and there's a big confrontation between these creatures and our heroes on top of a mountain, and I realized how strong and how physical these creatures were. I said, "That's the key. It's the opposite." The dementors don't have physical strength. Actually, I'm sure that if you slapped the hand, the hand would disintegrate. They're such corrupt organisms. So the difference is that the dementors are more ethereal, more metaphysical, more abstract. So I remember that Jo Rowling came in at one point and said that she thought that the dementors wouldn't work. This is when I thought about an amazing puppeteer from San Francisco called Basil Twist. He does puppeteer work underwater. He's amazing. He had a show here in New York many years ago and that's where I saw his stuff. What he does is puppeteer with fabrics under water. It's just the most amazing, beautiful effect. So we did some puppets and Basil went to London. We did tests. They were beautiful, but at the end of the day, they were not very practical. So we took the dementors to ILM and gave them Basil Twist's stuff as a reference. So pretty much what they did is computer generated, they recreated what we tried to do.

QUESTION: Did the kids' voices change at all during production?

CUARON: No. I think that Chris had to deal more with that stuff in the second film. Here, their voices had already broken more or less. So, we didn't really have to deal with that much. The kids, pretty much from the beginning to the end, yeah, they changed quite a lot, but not in a way that would be noticeable.

QUESTION: The clothing seemed more contemporary.

CUARON: That came out of a conversation with Jo Rowling. She said she thought it was great that they had uniforms and clothes, but I think that this is the first time they'd be wearing their street clothes. For me, as a director, it just gave me another tool to make character comments, through costumes.

QUESTION: Was it intentional to shoot sequences that looked like a black-and-white movie?

CUARON: From the get-go, together with the cinematographer and the production designer, we decided on a more monochromatic palate. We just tried to subdue a little bit the colors, but not take the extreme to black and white. It's this game of shadows and light.

QUESTION: What did you learn about Daniel Radcliffe from working with him?

CUARON: He's the coolest guy. What's something about Daniel and his family is that they keep a very, very, very healthy balance between work and school. They keep their priorities very, very, very straight. I think that helps a lot in making the amazing kid that Daniel is. As odd as Harry Potter is, he's still a normal kid. He's a normal, extraordinary kid. I have to say that [Daniel is] very eccentric. He has a wicked sense of humor. He's a like a sponge. He just absorbs absolutely everything. That would be okay, but what makes him so extraordinary is his sense of humor.

QUESTION: Any anecdote about working with him?

CUARON: Well, there are a lot of them. There's a scene with Michael Gambon, the scene where the kids are in the sleeping bag and Michael Gambon had a fart machine in the sleeping bag that he would operate with remote control. Michael Gambon, by the way, is such a wicked man. Everybody was taking in the seriousness of the situation and Michael would operate the thing and the funny thing is that the camera was in a close-up on Dan, and Dan was trying to keep it together, and you would see behind Dan little heads that would start getting up. The funny thing was that the first kid who got up was making the point, "It wasn't me. It was the girls."

QUESTION: Is Michael's sense of humor verbal or more in the form of practical jokes?

CUARON: He loves practical jokes. He's infamous because of that. Actually, this fart machine, he was performing and some friends of his were going to be at the play and he hid the fart machine under the seats of his friends. He's acting, he's performing Shakespeare or whatever and he used the remote on his friends sitting over there. He's such a wicked man. I love him.

QUESTION: Is it scary to be in another country and doing something that's so English?

CUARON: I feel responsible. No. That's what is fun and is eccentric, that Englishness. At the same time, the greatness of Harry Potter is so universal. It doesn't have boundaries. They're wizards, but their emotions are so human.

DANIEL RADCLIFFE AND EMMA WATSON
(Harry Potter and Hermione Granger)

QUESTION: How do you think you've changed over the course of the three movies?

EMMA WATSON: We've just been getting older.

DANIEL RADCLIFFE: I think that we've probably changed as actors as well. But I'm not conscious of it much. I haven't worked on the first one for three years now. So I can't really compare it to the third, because it's not very fresh in my mind.

QUESTION: Were you more confident this time around?

> **EMMA:** I think that you get more and more confident every time, really.
>
> **DANIEL:** That's because we've had more experience with directors.
>
> **EMMA:** It's funny because a lot of the crew who were on *Harry Potter I* are still doing *Harry Potter III*, so it's great.
>
> **DANIEL:** Yeah, and now *IV* as well. It's like a family.

QUESTION: Was it challenging adjusting to the different directorial styles of Chris Columbus and Alfonso Cuaron?

> **DANIEL:** Basically, I think that everything we learned with Chris we were now able to put into practice with a different director. I think that the reason Alfonso was able to do longer takes and more complicated shots was because with Chris we didn't have the experience or the focus to do that kind of stuff. We did with Alfonso. It is hard. It's more challenging, which is good because we're getting older and if we're not getting better there's no point in doing it, really. I think that we just learn more with each director and now with Mike Newell directing the fourth, I think that we'll learn even more as well.

QUESTION: Were you able to teach Alfonso anything about your characters?

> **EMMA:** One of the first things that he did when we met him is that he asked us to write an essay about our characters. Not just to help us, but to help him to see the character through our eyes. He gave us a lot of freedom with that as well, which was really good.
>
> **DANIEL:** I think it's quite important to mention that when we did the essay, we basically did exactly what our characters would've done in that situation. I wrote a page and it was fine. It was okay. It wasn't great. It's what Harry does. Rupert [Grint] didn't do it. Rupert forgot to do it. How many pages did you write?
>
> **EMMA:** It becomes a little bit more every single time [I tell it — Laughs]. I have big handwriting. I needed six pages.

QUESTION: Can you talk about how this has affected your ambitions? Are you going to go into politics?

Rupert, Emma and Daniel walk the red carpet at the New York premiere of Azkaban. (Diane Bondareff/AP Photo)

DANIEL: God help the nation if I become a politician. I really enjoy acting. I really love acting. I think it's really something I'd like to go on doing. Again, there's loads of other stuff, mainly music and writing and that, but I'd love to continue acting.

EMMA: I feel incredibly lucky to have been given the opportunity to be in such a fantastic film with tons of people. My ambitions couldn't even have dreamed of the scale and the greatness that Harry Potter is. So I feel really lucky about that. I love performing. I love being creative. There are so many aspects to the film world that even if I don't pursue acting, there'll be something in it for me that I'll end up doing. I'm just going to see what happens.

QUESTION: Anything from the book that didn't make it into the film that you kind of miss?

DANIEL: There was one scene in the third book. I can't actually remember what Harry said in it, but it was something, it was kind of him, I think. I may have this wrong because I haven't read the book in quite a while, but it was something where he comes out of Lupin's office and basically sits down. It's almost him just slightly despairing, but telling himself that he's got to get himself together if he wants to fight Voldemort. That's all I can remember. I think other than that, I got to play all the ones I wanted.

EMMA: I think that they did a really good job on this one. A lot was cut, but they did a great job of making sure that everything that was put in the film is really relevant to the plot. One of the things I think is really great about the film is that it's really fluid, it's really fast moving. I think that they did a really good job of getting everything that was important in there.

QUESTION: What was cut?

EMMA: Oh my goodness. There were a couple of fights with Ron that were cut. There was an awkward hug with Ron.

QUESTION: Why was it awkward?

EMMA: Well, just on the exterior, I think, Hermione and Ron spend the whole film just arguing with each other. Ron is convinced that Hermione's cat has eaten his rat. But I think that it's a bit of a cover-up really, because they have a bit of a soft spot for each other, and it's a classic love/hate relationship. You always tease the ones that you like.

QUESTION: How do you prepare for the tough scenes in the film, and was it difficult to clean it out of your system afterwards?

DANIEL: I don't know. Harry, being a teenager, has the same feelings as every other teenager basically, but because of his past I think that he feels those feelings of anger and loneliness more strongly. I think that was kind of hard for me. But because I'm obviously feeling the same things as him, I just basically exaggerated them and listened to music or something to get me in the right state of mind for filming and I just kind of hoped for the best.

EMMA: I have to say that Dan focused so hard on a lot of the scenes in this. One of the scenes he did, he was so into it he almost fainted.

DANIEL: I do this kind of stupid thing where I forget to breathe properly. I haven't done it lately.

QUESTION: You've been able to work with some amazing actors. . . .

DANIEL: It's amazing. I've watched I'd say 90 percent of Gary Oldman's films and I have so much respect for him as an actor. I think that he's one of the greatest actors of his generation and it was a complete inspiration to work with him. He's actually the nicest guy as well. He gave me a bass lesson. He's a really great bass player. It was so amazing for us to be working the [in] same room as Gary, David Thewlis, Alan Rickman and Timothy Spall all in one go. It was unbelievable.

EMMA: Daniel almost bit my head off at one point. He said, "Gary Oldman has been cast as Sirius Black," and I went, "Who?" Now I know that is the most terrible thing that I could possibly say, ever. Even though I didn't know him, just working with him, he did such a good job. He's great.

QUESTION: Did you learn anything working with these casts?

EMMA: Working with Emma Thompson, I had such a good time with her. I had really good fun with the scene that we did, because she was very creative and very involving with me, and she said, "Why don't we try this? Why don't we do it this way? Wouldn't it be good if we said this line here?" It was really flattering for her to involve me like that. It was really great and I had a really good time with her on that. I hope it gets some laughs in there.

QUESTION: How did you enjoy having your own story line in this film?

EMMA: I loved it. It's my favorite book. It's such a fantastic part for Hermione. She really comes into her own. I think that you see a really different side to her than you have in the other two. I think that it's much more personal, and this film has tested and challenged me. I've definitely enjoyed it the best out of three because of that.

QUESTION: What do you think about Michael Gambon's transition in the role of Dumbledore?

EMMA: I think that, obviously, it's very hard to follow Richard Harris. A lot of people thought that he was a perfect Dubmledore. He did a really, really great job. Instead of trying to make himself look exactly like Richard Harris, trying to copy him, he did his own thing with it. He's still Dumbledore, but he put a different spin on it.

DANIEL: He's more of a mischievous Dumbledore.

QUESTION: What's been the funniest thing you've experienced with a fan?

DANIEL: I went to MTV and I'm about to go again. It was the first time that I'd been there, and you've got the huge windows all around, and Carson Daly took me over to one of the windows and pointed down and there was a girl down there, and you've probably heard this before, but a girl was standing there wrapped in a towel and nothing else and holding a sign that said, "Nothing comes between me and Harry Potter." It was a Harry Potter towel as well.

July 2004

Penn State announced a Harry Potter–related program designed to tie in to *Prisoner of Azkaban* that would explore the world of science as presented in Harry's realm. Action Potential Science Experience camp director Rebecca Peterson said, "The Harry Potter books are capturing the imaginations of our young people, so we are providing them with a stimulating context for learning about the science behind the magic."

Feeling the film was immoral, the Chinese government banned

Prisoner of Azkaban, noting that it and other forms of media were having a corrupting effect on the youth of that country.

Edinburgh University bestowed an honorary degree on J.K. Rowling in recognition of her contributions to children's literature. The author enthused, "To receive such a tribute from the city I now call home, and to be in such distinguished company, means a lot to me." Elsewhere she announced that she would be offering a public reading at the ticket-only Edinburgh Book Festival. "This will be my fifth appearance at the Edinburgh Festival," she said. "There have been readings for each of the first four Potter books, and this time my appearance will coincide with the UK publication of *Order of the Phoenix* in paperback. I am looking forward to the event very much, because there will be a relatively small audience, which means I can see faces and take questions directly from the fans."

News of mentally disabled children being kept in cages in the Czech Republic shocked J.K. Rowling, who was vocal in the public demand for an investigation. "I am sure that I am not alone in feeling a deep sense of shock that a fellow member of the European Union like the Czech Republic could permit such abuses," Rowling exclaimed. In response, Czeck President Vaclav Klaus wondered to the media if the author knew more about the situation than she had read in the media, claiming that the situation had been exaggerated.

A Missouri post office was shut down in an anthrax scare caused by a letter sent by a Harry Potter fan that contained white powder. The sender intended it to be "floo powder," using talcum powder as a substitute. Oops!

Harry Potter fell under attack again, this time by a French professor who criticized the novels for their "individualism, excessive competition and a cult of violence."

British actress Miranda Richardson was announced for the role of *Daily Prophet* "journalist" Rita Skeeter in *Goblet of Fire*.

J.K. Rowling's official Web site reportedly received 220 million hits in just eight weeks. When she had launched the site, the author wrote, "Everything on here was written by me, J.K. Rowling. This is where I can tell you the truth about rumors or news stories, where I can share the extra information I haven't put in the books, where I can give you hints and clues about what's going to happen to Harry next and where I can announce I've finished book six. And, no, that's not going to happen very soon."

August 2004

A pair of prop diaries used in *Prisoner of Azkaban* were reportedly sold for more than $4,000.

British actor Ralph Fiennes was cast in one of the most important roles in the Potterverse, that of dark Lord Voldemort, in *Goblet of Fire*. "Voldemort is someone who knows no love," David Heyman notes. "He thinks of love as a flaw. He is the embodiment of pure evil. Someone who is powerful and attractive. Ralph is an actor of great depth, and he captures the complexity of Voldemort's charisma and darkness brilliantly."

At a public reading of her work in Scotland, J.K. Rowling offered some interesting albeit cryptic news items about her future Harry novels. Reported the *Guardian*, "The writer revealed a few morsels about her hero, including the revelation that he 'survives to book

He Who Is Named Ralph Fiennes, who was announced as Voldemort for Goblet of Fire, goofs around with Daniel Radcliffe. (Stuart Ramson/AP Photo)

seven,' although she refused to confirm whether he would grow up to be a wizard. She also revealed that there were two vital questions she had never been asked about the series that might help to unravel its mysteries. She said they should be asking themselves, "not 'Why did Harry live?' but 'Why didn't Voldemort die?'" "The second question, she added, is: "'Why didn't Dumbledore kill, or try to kill, Voldemort?'"

Despite rumors to the contrary, J.K. Rowling noted that the character of Gilderoy Lockhart was *not* based on her first husband, adding that "the living model is worse. He was a real shocker. I can say this quite freely because he will never in a million years dream that he is Gilderoy Lockhart."

On the release of the paperback edition of *Harry Potter and the Order of the Phoenix* on August 17, Scholastic was thrilled to learn that the tome had immediately hit the top of the bestseller lists.

According to *The Times of India*, director Mira Nair (*Vanity Fair*, *Monsoon Wedding*) was offered the directorial chair for film number five, *Harry Potter and the Order of the Phoenix*. Said Nair, "I read it over the weekend. I'm still deciding. I'm not letting all of this go to my head. I'm grounded. I practice detachment; it helps me keep my balance. My son Zoharan's excited. I've seen all the Harry Potter movies with him."

In China, *Order of the Phoenix* sold over 1.1 million copies in 2003, an astounding number for the territory.

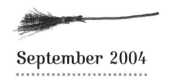

September 2004

On her official Web site, J.K. Rowling offered two lines from the forthcoming *Harry Potter and the Half-Blood Prince*. While some may view this as a cruel tease, for fans, any preview of the next novel was a cause for celebration.

Harry Potter novel artist Mary GrandPre agreed to do the poster for the 2005 Minnesota State Fair.

Digital Spy reported three new actors cast in *Goblet of Fire*: Shefali Chowdhury as Parvati Patil, Afshan Azad as Padma Patil and Angelica Mandy as Fleur Delacour's younger sister, Gabrielle.

Daniel Radcliffe was thrilled to see himself mentioned on the CD sleeve of a release from independent singer Ian Brown, formerly of '90s band Stone Roses.

Although Warner Brothers was deluged with requests from people wanting to audition for film number five, *Order of the Phoenix*, the studio stated that it was "far too early" to even think about such things.

Harry Potter reached its 200th language when J.K. Rowling's novels were translated into Gaelic.

J.K. Rowling's cousin, Ben, publicly expressed his anger that the author won't admit that she based the Harry Potter character on him and won't share any of her fortune with him. "When I read the first Harry Potter book," he said, "my jaw dropped. It was uncanny, far more than a coincidence. I know Jo based Harry on me. I can see so much of the young me in his character."

A leatherbound book containing a Harry Potter manuscript adorned by handwriting and drawings by J.K. Rowling went up for auction to support the 999 Club, a London-based charity providing local financial support. Noted J.K., "I support the club because of the way it works — supporting people from the local community, run by people from the local community, open to all."

October 2004

Alarms sounded globally when J.K. Rowling, on her Web site, was asked whether or not she planned on killing any more characters and she responded with, "Yes, sorry."

The Scottish band Franz Ferdinand made public the fact they would be doing some music for *Goblet of Fire*. Unfortunately tensions within the band resulted in their having to pull out.

Patrick Doyle was announced as the replacement for John Williams as composer for *Goblet of Fire*.

Despite Harry Potter's success, Mickey Mouse was the top earning fictional character of the year, according to *Forbes*.

Departing director Alfonso Cuaron expressed his opinion that Daniel Radcliffe, Emma Watson and Rupert Grint would remain in their roles through all seven films. "It would be amazing to have the whole series with the same kids," he offered. "It would be priceless. It would be something very special, for the ages. So far, they're holding up very good, the way that they are aging."

French director Jean-Pierre Jeunet (*Alien Resurrection, Amélie*) reportedly turned down the offer to direct *Order of the Phoenix*.

J.K. Rowling was given the top personality award by *Variety UK*, as part of the British Independent Film Awards.

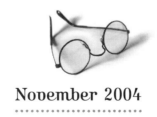

November 2004

Former James Bond Pierce Brosnan offered an interesting casting choice for a future 007: "For the next Bond, Colin Farrell would be great, but if you want to go ever younger, Daniel Radcliffe. Give him a few years. You can see it, can't you? He'll be great. From Harry Potter to Bond."

Miriam Margolyes let it be known that she was sad she would not be reprising the role of Professor Sprout in *Order of the Phoenix*, despite the fact that the character is in the book. "I am not making the fifth Harry Potter," the actress told the *Sun*. "They made a great mistake and cut my character."

Emma Watson was given the honor of lighting the special Christmas lights on Oxford Street in London. The event was also tied in to the DVD release of *Prisoner of Azkaban* and featured a Harry Potter light show.

Filming officially began on *Goblet of Fire* with the so-called sea of tents, all part of the Tri-Wizard tournament.

Michael Goldenberg, screenwriter of *Where the Wild Things Are*, *Peter Pan* and *Contact*, among others, was brought aboard to adapt *Order of the Phoenix*, while Steve Kloves went off to write and direct *The Curious Incident of the Dog in the Night-Time* for Harry producer David Heyman.

Apparently Gary Oldman was physically ill when he found out that J.K. Rowling had killed Sirius Black in *Order of the Phoenix*, limiting the number of films he could be in.

Daniel Radcliffe sent out a Christmas card featuring himself and numerous crewmembers underwater in the tank being used for the filming of part of *Goblet of Fire*.

Britain's Danny Holme, who was often said to have an amazing resemblance to Daniel Radcliffe's Harry Potter, actually won a national search for the best Harry Potter look-alike and was then invited to participate in an event tied in to the DVD release of *Prisoner of Azkaban.*

January 2005

The Harry Potter online scams continued, with some offering copies of the not-yet-published *Harry Potter and the Order of the Phoenix*. The online message claimed the book was available electronically only. "If you do not wish to wait for six months more, buy and start reading right now! Be the first to reveal all the secrets." The site was shut down as soon as authorities became aware of it. For the record, no electronic version of a Harry Potter novel has ever been made available.

David Yates, virtually unknown as a director in America, who directed the critically acclaimed BBC series *State of Play*, was officially announced as the director of the film adaptation of *Order of the Phoenix*. Enthused producer David Heyman, "I am thrilled that David Yates is going to direct. Not only does he have tremendous passion for the world of Harry Potter, but he is a great director with a keen visual sense who fills every frame with humanity and compassion for his characters."

J.K. Rowling gave birth to her third child, Mackenzie Jean Rowling Murray. Mackenzie is her second child with husband, Dr. Neil Murray.

When learning that children wanted owls as pets, J.K. Rowling was quick to point out that this was not a good idea. "If anybody has been influenced by my book to think an owl would be happiest shut in a small cage and kept in a house, I would like to take this opportunity to say as forcefully as I can: You are wrong. The owls in Harry Potter books were never intended to portray the true behavior or preference of real owls," she wrote on her Web site.

J.K. Rowling's lawyers made note of the fact that they were exploring whether or not they would sue the U.S. army for its Harry Potter–inspired illustration that appeared in their official publication, *Preventive Maintenance Monthly.*

February 2005

Preorders for the sixth Harry Potter novel, *Half-Blood Prince*, had, according to Amazon.co.uk, topped 100,000. The book's publication date was announced as July 16.

While speaking to the *Melbourne Herald Sun*, Rupert Grint expressed his confidence he would be returning for film five. "There's no reason, really, why we couldn't go on," he said. "I don't know about the others, but I want to go on."

Word leaked out that the names of the film crew would appear on gravestones in a *Goblet of Fire* cemetery sequence.

At the Visual Effects Society Awards, *Harry Potter and the Prisoner of Azkaban* took home the top prize for Outstanding Visual Effects.

Rumors were making the rounds that Elizabeth Hurley was being pursued for a role in *Order of the Phoenix*, but these turned out to be false.

Lawyer-turned-author John Grisham admitted that the end of his reign on the top of the bestseller lists kind of bummed him out. "I was number one for a long time," he said. "I tried to act like it was no big deal, but I kind of miss it." He was dethroned, of course, by J.K. Rowling's Harry Potter novels.

March 2005

Scholastic released the cover for *Half Blood Prince* on the eighth of the month. Explained artist Mary GrandPre, "For the cover, the mood of the art is truly eerie. I wanted the colors to be strong and I chose upward lighting and dramatic shadows to convey a kind of surreal place and time." In the image, Harry and Dumbledore are looking into a basin that is emitting a green light.

Electronic Arts and Warner Brothers announced a *Goblet of Fire* game that would complement the film and feature the likenesses of Daniel Radcliffe, Emma Watson and Rupert Grint.

Scholastic reported that the forthcoming *Half-Blood Prince* was shattering all records with an initial print run of 10.8 million copies.

J.K. Rowling admitted that she thought the new book was the best so far. "Even if nobody else likes it — and some won't — I know it will remain one of my favorites in the series. Ultimately you have to please yourself before you please anyone else."

Academics from all over the world were expected to gather in Britain between July 29 and 31 to participate in the first Harry

Half-Blood Prince arrived in bookstores with a dire warning that carried serious consequences if the boxes were opened early. (Jim Sugar/Corbis)

Potter Conference. Noted the BBC, "Professors and academics are involved in the event at Reading University, looking at topics such as the social issues of the wizarding community. Lighthearted events include a mock trial of potions master Severus Snape and a Hogwarts-style banquet. But those aged under 18 are not able to take part, despite the fact J.K. Rowling's books are aimed at children. Seminar topics being discussed around the books include mythic symbols, alchemy and religious identity."

April 2005

Fourteen people in Britain were convicted of using fake names to obtain millions in government funds. Among the fake names used was Harry Potter.

ABC announced that *Harry Potter and the Chamber of Secrets* would be airing on May 7. An extra treat for fans would be behind-the-scenes footage and clips from the forthcoming *Goblet of Fire*.

May 2005

IMAX and Warner Brothers announced that *Goblet of Fire* would be issued in the large-screen format in addition to regular format.

Speaking to *USA Today*, Daniel Radcliffe confirmed he would be returning as Harry Potter in *Order of the Phoenix*, and he also admitted that he had not gone back to watch his younger self in the earlier Potter films. "I kind of contemplated watching the first, then I decided I sort of valued my sanity a little too much. I think it would be far too strange and I would be self-conscious about what I do now."

The BBC reported that at 12:01 a.m. on July 16, a global media competition would allow 70 people to attend a reading from *Half-Blood Prince* by J.K. Rowling at Edinburgh Castle. Offered the BBC, "The lucky children will travel up the Scottish capital's historical Royal Mile in horse-drawn carriages to the Castle Esplanade for the event, which will be broadcast live worldwide on TV and radio. The youngsters, who must be aged from 8 to 16, will return to the oak-beamed Great Hall of the castle later on the Saturday for a Hogwarts-style banquet. On the Sunday, the winners will then have the opportunity to be cub reporters and question Rowling, in what the author has promised will be the book's only news conference."

About two months before the publication of *Half-Blood Prince*, speculation was running high that Professor Dumbledore would perish in the book.

June 2005

Potterinsanemania — All things Harry were obviously getting out of hand, with a reporter from Britain's *Sun* being shot at by someone who tried selling him an illegal copy of the *Half-Blood Prince* novel for nearly $100,000, and somehow J.K. Rowling's lawyers got a court injunction designed to stop *anyone* with advanced knowledge of the new novel from saying anything publicly about it. Nice to have clout like that!

Emerson Sparts who runs the Web site www.mugglenet.com and Melissa Anelli of www.the-leaky-cauldron.org were awakened by phonecalls from J.K. Rowling inviting both of them to come "across the pond" to interview her. A rare opportunity indeed. "When the phone rang at 8 a.m.," Anelli related to the *Times*, "I must have said, 'Oh my God!' forty-eight times."

The success of Harry Potter in print and on the big screen inspired a tourism boom for fans wanting to check out real-life locations that relate to Harry.

Tie-in merchandise for the publication debut of *Half-Blood Prince* was cut down considerably as the expected boom of sales did not happen when *Order of the Phoenix* was published.

Amazon.com preorders for *Half-Blood Prince* were expected to top 1.3 million copies.

Oregon's Natalie Jacobsen, age 15, spent a year writing her own 804-page Harry Potter novel with the hopes of showing it to J.K. Rowling. "I really love the books," said Jacobsen, "and I want to be an author when I'm older. I went to the London premiere of the last Harry Potter film to try to meet J.K. Rowling, but it didn't happen. So now I've come to Edinburgh and I really want to show her my book."

July 2005

Nigel Newton of Bloomsbury said that since Harry Potter had been turned down by every other publisher, the character owes at least part of his success to Nigel's daughter, to whom he had given a sample of Rowling's manuscript. "She came down from her room an hour later glowing," Newton told the *New Zealand Herald*, "saying, 'Dad, this is so much better than anything else.' She nagged and nagged me in the following months, wanting to see what came next." *Everyone* knows the answer to that one.

Bloomsbury announced that Braille editions of *Half-Blood Prince* would be available at the same time as regular publication. This was a first for the series.

Harry fans were encouraged to purchase copies of *Order of the Phoenix* from Canadian sellers, the book being printed there on recycled paper.

As J.K. Rowling was getting ready to celebrate her 40th birthday on July 31, it was reported that despite her great success, she had not really changed as a person. Pointed out Scholastic's Arthur A. Levine, "It's a testament to her character, more than anything else, that she's remained true to herself. She has managed to maintain her perspective. I think that takes a great deal of effort."

British teenager Owen Jones, 14, won the chance to be the only person to interview J.K. Rowling on UK television. In that eventual interview, Rowling offered her thoughts on ending the series of novels. "I am dreading it in some ways," she admitted. "I do love writing the books and it is going to be a shock, a profound shock to me. Even though I have known it is coming for the past fifteen years, I have known that the series would end, I think it will still be a shock."

When a Canadian bookseller sold copies of *Order of the Phoenix* ahead of time, a judge ruled that the buyers could not say anything about it. One additional copy was inadvertently sold in America.

In a letter written several years ago, Cardinal Josef Ratzinger, before becoming Pope Benedict XVI, expressed his opinion that Harry Potter was decidedly anti-Catholic.

On the verge of *Half-Blood Prince*'s publication, *USA Today* reported that nearly 2,000 bookstores in the U.S. were planning Harry Potter parties in which kids could dress up like Harry, make wands and place temporary lightning tattoos on their foreheads.

In its first 24 hours on sale, *Half-Blood Prince* sold 6.9 million copies.

Reviewed Molly Griffin of the *Observer*, "The penultimate book in J.K. Rowling's massively popular series deals brilliantly with the dif-

An aspiring Harry Potter holds a copy of Half-Blood Prince *in a bookstore in Calcutta. (Pival Adhikary/epa/Corbis)*

ficult task of setting up the final tale of the boy wizard's adventures. While not necessarily the best book of the series, it effectively brings together many of the multiple plot strings that arose in earlier volumes and pushes them forward for the final novel, which is no easy task. This book reveals the care and attention to detail with which Rowling planned the Potter series from the beginning."

August 2005

Bootleg copies of *Half-Blood Prince* went on sale in China three months prior to the official publication of the translated version.

J.K. Rowling joined Stephen King, Nick Hornby and Bob Dylan as writers nominated for Quills awards in the U.S.

British director Terry Gilliam told Celebrity Spider that he was still annoyed at not having the chance to direct the first Harry Potter film, which he said he had been led to believe would be his. He also dismissed the Chris Columbus efforts: "[His] versions are terrible. Just dull. Pedestrian."

September 2005

One rumor making the rounds was that Daniel Radcliffe was one of two actors being considered for a series of films based on the *Young Bond* novels. There was no basis to these rumors.

CBBC Newsround covered the fact that a three-dimensional portrait of J.K. Rowling was being unveiled at London's National Portrait Gallery. "It shows J.K. sitting at a desk in a bare room," the report goes on, "with a writing pad in front of her, along with three boiled eggs, to represent her three children." At the unveiling, Rowling herself said, "This genuinely is the first time that I have seen this and I love it. . . . This shows more of me than any photo has ever shown."

J.K. Rowling made audio versions of her novels available on iTunes. As the author wrote on her Web site, "Many Harry Potter fans have been keen for digital access for a while, but the deciding factor for me in authorizing the new version is that it will help combat the growing [number of] incidents of piracy in this area."

Rowling also warned fans of fake signed Harry Potter items being offered on eBay.

J.K. Rowling loved Stuart Pearson Wright's portrait of her that was unveiled at the National Portrait Gallery in September 2005. (Fiona Hanson/PA/CP Photo)

Emma Watson expressed her concern that other roles could be difficult to get. "My biggest fear is getting stereotyped," she said. "I want to do other things. But I would hate to have another actress in the role. There is so much of me in her. Of course J.K. Rowling wrote the character, but in film terms I had a part in creating her."

In an interview with the Los Angeles *Daily News*, director Mike Newell expressed his belief that there would be a different feel to *Goblet of Fire* because he was the first Englishman to direct an entry in the series. "Whether anyone will notice, I don't know, but I hope it has a kind of authenticity. And it's a little darker than the others, because these kids are growing up, and they have to face stuff that they haven't had to before. But the real thing about it is that it's a terrific adventure story and a really good thriller."

Celebrity Spider featured an interview with Ralph Fiennes in which he said that his work on *Harry Potter* was changing his life. "No matter what I've done in the past," he said, "now that I've played Voldemort, nothing else will ever match it again. I don't know if I'm going to play Voldemort in all four remaining films, but even now, every time I go to the supermarket, people come up to me and ask if I'm really 'he who must not be named.' I can see *Harry Potter* taking over my life."

Sales for all of the Harry Potter novels had exceeded 300 million copies.

More than 1,000 Harry fans attended the Witching Hour symposium on J.K. Rowling's world held in Salem, Massachusetts. This was only the latest in a series of symposiums held in different states between 2003 and the present. In describing the symposium, www.witchinghour.org offered, "A chief aim of 'The Witching Hour' is to foster dialogue between academics and fans of the series. Harry Potter online fan culture — which includes original stories and art inspired by Rowling's world — is rich and varied. It is already enormous and is still growing. For instance, one of the major fan fiction archive sites boasts nearly 200,000 new stories, contributed by writers from around the globe. And the fans themselves will be sharing their creative endeavors, reading from their fiction and displaying their artwork that features Harry and his friends — and enemies. Throughout the course of the conference, both fans and scholars will be able to interact [with] and learn from each other's perspectives, to gain a deeper understanding of the series."

J.K. Rowling took home a Quill Book Award for Best Children's Book for *Half-Blood Prince*.

Actress Imelda Staunton confirmed she would be playing

Professor Dolores Umbridge in the film version of *Order of the Phoenix*.

October 2005

Producer David Heyman announced that Steve Kloves would be returning to Hogwarts to write the adaptation of *Half-Blood Prince* after having to miss out on *Order of the Phoenix*.

The BBC reported that the Weasley's flying car as seen in *Chamber of Secrets* had been stolen from the studio it was kept in.

A UK Sci-Fi Channel poll voted Harry Potter the Greatest Screen Fantasy Hero of All Time.

November 2005

In an interview with London's *Daily Record*, Daniel Radcliffe pointed out that there was more to him than just Harry Potter, a point he would be proving at the end of the year by taking on the role of an orphan named Maps in the film *December Boys*. "He's very different from Harry," said Radcliffe. "He doesn't have Harry's zest for life. But I don't feel pressure. I just want to do the best job I can."

Smitten fans await the arrival of Daniel Radcliffe and Rupert Grint at the New York premiere of Goblet of Fire. *(Andrew Gombert/epa/Corbis)*

Just before *Harry Potter and the Goblet of Fire* hit theaters, the *New York Post* noted: "As expected, many scenes in the massive book are deleted, combined or shortened to make the film flow smoother and faster." The article went on to detail some "surprising" changes, the most surprising of which "is in the film's first scene, when the character out to kill Harry is revealed immediately. In the book, that character is kept a secret until the very end, when he is unveiled in a page-turning plot twist."

Speaking to *USA Today* about *Goblet of Fire*, director Mike Newell pointed out, "What Harry is up against now is an utterly malignant human creature. This is not a three-headed dog. This is the ultimate evil itself. Voldemort is a lot more savage and cruel than any invented creature could be."

In a separate article, *USA Today* credited the works of J.K. Rowling as the reason sales of science fiction and fantasy books had climbed 8.5 percent in a period of five years, which was nearly twice as much as the rate for all consumer books.

NASA actually transmitted *Goblet of Fire* to the International Space Station at the request of astronaut Bill McArthur.

Twelve-year-old Breeze Gardner, whose mom is confined to a wheelchair due to MS, wrote to J.K. Rowling to request an auto-graphed copy of *Harry Potter and the Half-Blood Prince* that she could auction off for charity. Amazingly, that's exactly what she received and, according to the *Daily Record*, the rare volume was expected to go for about $10,000 in auction.

Director Mike Newell gave an interview in which he explained that it had been his hope to deal with a darker adolescent tone in *Goblet of Fire*, but, "I found, to my horror, that Alfonso had gotten there before me and with great style and determination." In the same interview he added, "The children are growing up, and that's what the basic story is. You have to be true to growing up in an abstract way and to these kids in a particular way."

Harry Potter and the Goblet of Fire was released on November 18, 2005, scoring $102,685,961 in its opening weekend. Domestically it would gross $290,013,036, with a foreign take of $602,200,000, for a global total of $892,213,036.

Cast and crew of *Goblet of Fire* met with the press shortly before the film's release, and what follows are edited transcripts of those sessions.

MIKE NEWELL AND DAVID HEYMAN
(Director and Producer)

QUESTION: How does this film differ from the previous Harry Potter films?

MIKE NEWELL: For me, it is that I think in the previous films, because of the age of the people, the scale of the challenge to the leading character has been limited. He's had a basilisk to deal with, he's had this problem, that problem, but he's never actually been challenged in his self. He's never had to put up or shut up. He's always had the group to rely on, and now in this one, he's older, he's more conscious, so he knows much more what's happening to him, and he knows when Voldemort says in the graveyard, "Do you want to take it in the back or do you want to take it in the front? But you're gonna get it, whichever way," and what Harry says is "Alright, I'll show you." And he comes out, and he's ready for a fight, and he knows that it's a fight to the death. And he has the moral courage to do it. Of course there are lots and lots of wonderful new things about this, like the jokes on growing up and girls and, oh God, how do we dance, and all of those things. But the big difference is that the challenge is kind of a moral one, and he may not survive it.

DAVID HEYMAN: And for Harry, when we went and spoke to Jo [Rowling] the first time, it was very important to her that the theme that would continue through it all was to stand up and be counted. Even if you think you might not win, you have to stand up for what you believe in.

NEWELL: David [Heyman] took me up to see J.K. Rowling two years ago now. And she talked about just that, she talked about these moral challenges, and she was brilliant about it, and I took a great deal away from that.

HEYMAN: That's really the essence that Mike [Newell] sort of took from the beginning, right through [to] the end: it is a thriller, another change. The world has expanded, we've got two new schools coming in, we have the first interaction with the opposite sex, both the good and the awkward and uncomfortable sides of that, that begin at thirteen, fourteen, and never go away. But its heart, as Mike said, is this moral stuff. Harry is now fourteen, he's much more of an individual than he's ever been before. He's becoming more who he is.

NEWELL: It's terribly interesting, isn't it?

HEYMAN: What the Dark Lord is grooming him to be.

NEWELL: Both you and I are taking Emma [Watson] as a sort of honorary boy. But of course Emma now gets to be a young woman, which is something that I personally am very proud of, because I thought that she allowed herself to be very vulnerable. She could so easily have said, "Well I'm Hermione and I'm going to be this and that," but she was very, very allowing of a vulnerability, and not knowing, and not being kind of cool. And I was very pleased by that. Just as in number three, there's this hugely satisfying moment where she hits Malfoy, *bop*. So there is in this one this wonderful moment where she's unsure and insecure.

HEYMAN: I think the kids are growing as actors, and Mike is benefiting from them having had two years with two films with Chris [Columbus] and one film with Alfonso [Cuaron]. Mike is one of the great directors of actors, and the kids are challenged. He didn't let them rest one minute or get comfortable; he pushed and pushed and pushed, and I think the performances show it.

QUESTION: What is the challenge of using some of these great British actors as basically background to Harry's story?

NEWELL: It's actually a problem. And I think that the way that we attacked it, was that even though each of them — Maggie Smith, Alan Rickman, Mike Gambon, Robbie Coltrane — is now estab-

Mike Newell, director of Goblet of Fire, *shows Voldemort how it's done.*
(Kevork Djansezian/AP Photo)

lished, there's no more exploration for the audience to do of those characters. Indeed they mustn't change, in a way. And so what you have to do is to find a kind of lapidary way of using these tiny little bits, which will show you parts of these characters that you've never seen before. And so you've never seen Hagrid in love before, and a very wonderful thing it is, too. She did this thing at rehearsal, nobody could believe it — this is Frances de la Tour — and they found themselves opposite one another, and of course they're both of them great natural comedians, and so it was wonderful seeing these two people being kind of awkward and blushing and retiring with one another. And then suddenly she leant forward and does what she actually does in the scene in the movie, she picks something out of his beard, and we all thought, "Oh wasn't that wonderful!" And then, God help us, she ate it. [Laughs] So you know, those little things, and a tiny moment like that will keep those characters alive, but yes, it's something you have to work at — it's difficult.

QUESTION: Working with Dumbledore in particular has changed in that this is the first time we're seeing things beyond his control.

NEWELL: Yes, that was really interesting, because Michael was very game for that. I think that he had not wanted to be the same figure that Richard Harris had been, who was a figure of tremendous Olympian authority. He'd wanted something different to do simply because he wasn't Richard Harris. And what he found in this one was that Dumbledore is fallible. And not omnipotent, and indeed is behind the game, and a great deal of what he does is about being inadequate, rather than super-adequate, which of course is much more interesting to play.

QUESTION: Mike, did you have much knowledge of the movies and books prior to being approached for this one?

NEWELL: Yes, I'd read one book, the first book; and I'd seen both the films before I was approached, and so I was hoping to be approached. I was therefore educated pretty reasonably when I was approached, but then of course I started to particularly watch the films, obsessively. And I can still in my sleep do close textual analysis on numbers one, two, and three.

HEYMAN: And Alfonso was very generous.

NEWELL: Yeah he was, actually. As I'm sure Chris would've been.

HEYMAN: As Mike has been with David Yates [*Order of the Phoenix*]. And Alfonso now, you know, engaged Mike in discussions about the process and visual effects and allowed him to see the film early, just as Mike did with David Yates. And David Yates has seen a rough cut of the film, so it's been really great. By the way, I wanted Mike from the very beginning.

QUESTION: This film is so different from the previous ones. Do you think it's

Producer David Heyman had secured the rights to the Harry Potter films before the books had become a phenomenon. (Ian West/PA/CP Photo)

not just a kids' movie anymore?

    NEWELL: Not a kid movie for me. It's an adventure story, and it's a huge entertainment. Warner Brothers absolutely hated me saying this, so I'm gonna say it. But for me it had all the kind of variety that a Bollywood movie has. It's just — oh no, he said it! [Laughs] But at any rate, it's a huge broad-based entertainment, but above everything else, David is habitually very modest about this stuff, but he was very, very good when he first approached me, because what he said was, "You must read the book, and if you find a way of doing the book, then you must tell us what that is. You mustn't come because it's a franchise, you mustn't come because it's the most famous children's film that's ever been, you mustn't come for this, that, and the other reason, you've got to be able to see how to make a seven-hundred-and-fifty-page book into a single movie." And we then had one of the meetings made in heaven, where we talked about the thing as being a thriller. Because that's what I found in it; I thought that it was an absolutely God-given thriller — and then I convinced him.

HEYMAN: For me, the books are not children's books. I think that's a misconception. I think the books are books that appeal to . . . maybe you could say *children* of all ages, but I think they appeal to people of all ages. I think there is something for everybody in them, and I think with this film, each book is getting more mature than the one that preceded it, because it's also dealing with a different age, a different year in Harry's life. And in this one, Harry's fourteen, so there're different issues, there's greater complexity, and I think that really shows in the film, because the film is true to that script. The other thing is, when you bring in a director like Mike Newell, just as when you bring in a director like Alfonso Cuaron, they're not cookie cutters. You don't bring in a director like Mike Newell and tell him "Well, you've got to make a film just like Chris Columbus." I mean, it would be foolish. So for me, I look at this film, and I see Mike Newell — I mean, I see Jo Rowling, but I see Mike Newell written all over it, and that's really exciting to me. Just as I saw with Alfonso, I saw Alfonso written all over *Prisoner.*

NEWELL: Yes, I saw that with Alfonso and with Chris.

HEYMAN: I think it's really important. And I'm sure that David Yates will imbue the fifth [film] with the same. And it's really exciting for me, this is a big, generous, smart, funny, thriller.

QUESTION: Are you happy with the PG-13 rating?

HEYMAN: Very much so. And I'm very happy with the 12A in the UK. One, I think it will be good for the slightly older audience, and two, I think that we had to be . . . it shows that we've been faithful to the material. The books do not talk down to an audience. The audience reaches for the books, and I think the films do the same. We don't patronize our audience. The film is very much in the spirit; it's not literally faithful, but it is in the spirit, it is truly faithful to the spirit of what Jo has written, and that's really exciting to me.

NEWELL: One of the challenges was that, of course, everything goes back to the book, always. And that's where the audience begins as well. And so as the audience, which began with the first book, progresses through two and three, they get to four, and they see that it's a different kind of animal; it's a much tougher beast than the others. And if you don't get a PG-13, in a way, then that audience that began with number one and is now fourteen, fifteen, sixteen — or sixty-four, whatever — will kind of want to know why you are infantilizing the situation. Of course David says these are not children's books, these are kind of adult stories, with a very strong moral aim and view. So with PG-13 they can believe; without it, I'm not sure they can.

QUESTION: How does this film rank personally for you?
    NEWELL: I truly mean this: I can't stand myself sometimes. David has seen me in rushes, where I simply can't bear the ordinariness of what I do. And I always feel that about every [film].
    HEYMAN: Even when it's extraordinary?
    NEWELL: Doesn't matter. And I always hate the end result. And this time, and it may be a very bad sign, I don't know, but this time I *don't* hate it; this time I think it's what I tried to do, what we all tried to do. Which was to make this wonderful, terrifying thriller ride. And so it pleases me very much, and that's a better way of answering your question.

QUESTION: What were you expecting in terms of working with the kids?
    NEWELL: My worst fear was that they would have realized that these films were stories in which they absolutely were the stars. Now in most children's films, that's not true. Most children's films, they are a sort of a little bolt on a third of the story while the weight is still taken by the adults. In that way, *Mary Poppins* is not quite a children's story, it's an adult's story. But that's not the case here. This is a story in which the children are stars, and that can do terrible things to [child actors]. And miraculously, mostly because of the way they're

Joining the three regulars for Goblet of Fire *were Katie Leung (Cho Chang),*
Stanislav Lanevski (Viktor Krum), Clémence Poésy (Fleur Delacour) and
Robert Pattinson (Cedric Diggory). (INFGoff.com/CP Photo)

handled by the production and also because they've got very good
parents — a good kid has good parents — they haven't [been badly
affected]. They know exactly what they're worth, but they have not
become impossible, and so they're still loose, and they're still curious,
and they're still prepared to have a go at anything. Before we began
shooting, we had two weeks of acting classes, and the reason we did
this was that I was very anxious that the established characters
would not dominate the newcomers. Many of whom had never acted
before. The Chinese girl had never acted before, the two little Indian
girls had never acted before. And I didn't want them feeling that they
were secondary citizens, and so we had these two weeks where what
we did was we played, we did physical exercises, we did improvisa-
tional exercises, so on and so forth. And by the end of that, everybody was loose in one another's company, and there was no rank
structure. It wasn't that Dan outshone anybody else, they were all the
same. And they were prepared to do that, which is a very wonderful
thing. And it shows. What you've got now is an ensemble, rather
than a top-down pyramid structure.

HEYMAN: I think in this film more than the previous three films, there was a sense of community amongst the kids. They all were playing and joking and laughing, and there was a lot more hanging out, and Dan, Rupert, and Emma were all part of that. And so it's a much more extended community, much more like school life than I think it's ever been.

NEWELL: That's a good point, actually. I hadn't thought of that, but you're right, it was much more like the kind of loose relationships that you would build up in school, but much bigger.

HEYMAN: And I have to say, we are blessed. The three kids who could, as Mike said, so easily be brats, are not. They want to learn, they want to get better at what they do, they are enthusiastic still, and they have a lot of fun doing it. I think partly the rehearsal that Mike had them do, but also by their very nature, they are nonjudgmental, open people, who are good people from the top down. I think Mike will attest to this. Though the buck always stops with him, ultimately, it's a very democratic environment. It's one in which everybody has a voice, sometimes too much of one [laughs], but everybody does.

NEWELL: I agree. The trouble is, you can't start to play that game unless you play that game all the way through. I agree with you.

HEYMAN: It's a place in which everybody is welcome, and it's a very safe place for kids to be; everybody to be.

QUESTION: How frequently did you consult with J.K. Rowling about the story line?

NEWELL: Actually, you should ask David, because this is an absolutely key function of David's. Jo Rowling appears to me to be quite extraordinarily hands-off. Everybody says, "Oh we're surprised to hear that, we thought that she was very controlling." Well, I speak as I find — she wasn't with me. I don't think it's in her nature, I don't think she's like that. The danger, of course, is straying too far from the novels because you could lose Jo Rowling, at which point you lose the audience. Because they come in the end for her. And she was very, very sweet, she was very available, she's not the best returner of a phone call that I've come across, but she was fine. She gave me very clear things, when I needed them, like what did the Avada Kedavra curse actually do when it hit you. But she also had this very strong view of how the story fit into this seven-book arc. Beyond that, she didn't control at all. But of course it was to David's credit that she was brought into the process just as much as he knew she wanted to be, and not an inch more. I mean, how does that work?

HEYMAN: Jo is the most generous of collaborators. She sees each and every draft of the screenplay. We want to do that, because, one, I made a promise at the beginning that we would be true; but two, because we'd be fools to be otherwise. And so we show her each draft, and we also don't want to do anything that will disrupt the books. Also, she has incredible knowledge. What's in the books is just the surface of what she knows: she has notebook upon note-book of more material that doesn't find its way into the books. I think one of the reasons for the success of the books is because the universe is so clearly thought through. There was one very significant change that we made, and we called Jo to ask her about it, because it was major, and it had to do with Barty Crouch Jr. being present in that very first scene in the film. With Voldemort and Peter Pettigrew. The scene takes place in the novel, but Barty Crouch Jr. is not in it. And the reason why we wanted that is because we needed Barty Crouch Jr. to be more a recognizable and formidable presence when you got to the end, when Moody turns back into him. And without that, the only time you would have seen him would have been in the flashback, when he didn't look exactly like he did at the end. So I called Jo and asked her, and I think she said that's absolutely fine. What she loved about the third film, she hasn't yet seen the fourth, but what she loved about the third film was that it was true to the spirit, that it made changes, but it made changes in the spirit of the work. That's what she has felt so far in the process, the inclusive process of the script. I know she'll feel it when she sees the film. She was meant to see it last week, but some personal matters came up and she couldn't.

QUESTION: How did the young actors handle all the physical challenges?

NEWELL: Well, Dan's a very brave boy. He really is a brave boy. He's a rotten swimmer, or he was, when this began. And he had great trepidation, and he came to me, about the swimming, and there wasn't any way around it — he had to swim. He had to spend huge amounts of time underwater in the tank, and apart from anything else, he was by no means sure that he had the physical resources to do that. You couldn't say that he was frightened of it, but [fear] was only a step away. And nonetheless, he knuckled down, and he did what he had to do.

HEYMAN: Actually, on the first film, when we began the process, Dan was not a physical boy. And he wanted to be more physical, and actually we encouraged that. We put him together with our stunt team, and he is now a jock of sorts. I mean, his body has changed, he's really much more physical than he ever was. But lunch break for example, several times a week, he'll go down to the gym and work out. It's not something we're asking him to do, he just loves to do it. At times he likes to do his own stunts, he's very brave, as Michael said. In the underwater scene, he logged forty-one hours on his log book.

QUESTION: What role does screenwriter Steve Kloves play in the continuity of the series?

HEYMAN: Steve Kloves is one of the great experiences for me, one of the great joys of this entire series. I think he's one of the best writers writing, he is a brilliant adapter in the sense that he's able to retain the voice of the author that he's adapting. He did it with Michael Chabon with *Wonder Boys* and I think he's done it in the four Potter films that he's written. He is a fantastic writer who has a keen sense of character, and really understands the voice of the actors he is writing for, and he can write with great emotion and at the same time also, great humor. He is not doing the fifth because he is writing another project for me called *The Curious Incident of the Dog in the Night-Time*, which I thought he [might] direct, however he read the sixth [Potter] book and couldn't stay away, so he's going to come back and write the sixth. Michael Goldenberg is writing the fifth, he is another writer that I actually talked to about the first film, and he's doing a fantastic job. You can never make a good film out of a bad script. You most certainly can make a bad one out of a good one, but the key is to have a good script, and I really believe that Steve Kloves, on each of the four films, has given us a really good script. He's also a man, and Mike can speak to this a little bit, who writes without ego. It's great when you sit in the script meeting with him, because you can say anything, and he's thought through everything. That doesn't mean that he doesn't defend what he has, but he does it in a way which explains the reason why he has done what he has done, but it's always open to changes. He also has an encyclopedic knowledge of the world, and he and Jo are very much on the same wavelength.

NEWELL: It was the happiest collaboration I think I've ever had, certainly as an adapter. And he never gets in your way. I am one of those who will want stuff to be written and rewritten and re-rewritten. He would never, ever complain, he would always see why, and he would always dig down into his personal mine of stuff, and come up with wonderful things. I can't tell you how happy I was with him.

DANIEL RADCLIFFE, EMMA WATSON AND RUPERT GRINT

(Harry, Hermione and Ron)

QUESTION: How did you identify with the character growing up in this film?

DANIEL RADCLIFFE: For me, it's great because there is so much pressure on the films now to be better, especially after the third one, which for me was great. There was an awareness that we had to work really hard, to go further with it and to make it better, because otherwise people would be very disappointed, and so for me it is also a lot of fun, loads of fun playing Harry as he's getting older. I think that when we [start with] Harry's tenth birthday [in the book] — it's almost as if [it's] in real life and not just in the stories, but people sort of grow extra emotions. That's partly to do with hormones and all the trouble that they cause, and then partly just a thing about growing up. You have other assets, and so it's fun playing that in Harry as he grows older.

EMMA WATSON: And then there's been a lot of speculation about whether we're going to outgrow our parts or that the films will take longer, but it actually works out pretty well because each film takes about a year. Obviously that coincides with us doing our year at school. So we're pretty much growing alongside them. Sometimes everything that we're going through, in some instances, they are too.

DANIEL: There is always this thing of whether we will get too old for the part. People actually play a lot younger than they are in real life. I don't think that it's as big an issue as a lot of people make it out to be.

RUPERT GRINT: I think that all of the characters have sort of grown. I think Ron was a bit more moody in this one. There's a few of those things, and I enjoyed doing it.

QUESTION: As you get older and more successful, is there a risk of you guys becoming party animals?

EMMA: Hopefully not.

DANIEL: I'm planning on buying twenty Porsches and crashing them all just to be extravagant. I don't think so. I think that it's a really good thing that we haven't gotten like that. Because the characters are so well known and iconic, if we'd been going out — basically if we'd gone to every party under the sun that we were invited to, it would've been hard for people to divorce what they see in the film from what they see in magazines and stuff. So I think that would've been a mistake, which is why I think that we basically only go to the premieres.

EMMA: I think that we do have a kind of responsibility to that as well. I don't think that we are the party animals.

DANIEL: I certainly quite enjoy not having the high profile thing. I quite like that, because I sort of feel like I'm fooling people, because it's this massive thing and yet it's still quite a low-key thing. I feel I'm tricking everyone [laughs].

QUESTION: What is it like when you return to school between films?

EMMA: You do get some funny looks, but after a while they just accept the fact that you're there all the time, and that's how I like it.

DANIEL: The only thing that I would sort of say is that basically when you get back to school, as Emma said, originally there's a sort of novelty factor. People are going, "Ah, look who it is. It's that person." It's like you're sort of running along with an extra arm or something, but after a few weeks or something it sort of settles down and they go, "Oh. That's just the kid with the extra arm." So it doesn't seem to affect everyone so much. I was at school when the third film came out and then it got sort of fever pitch again, sort of mad. But it's not really a problem.

RUPERT: I'm finished with school now, and so I don't really get that.

QUESTION: How would you describe the bond between your characters?

DANIEL: What's quite nice about the thing that goes on between Harry and Ron in this one, and the tension, is that it's funny for someone looking in on it, but to them it's absolutely serious and they're really angry at each other. Each of them feels that they have both behaved in a really bad way, and so it's sort of like they feel betrayed by the other. It's also mutual blame. They're both to blame for how they are acting with each other, but to someone else on the outside sort of watching it, it's quite funny, because in the long run it's actually quite trivial what they're arguing about, as a lot of arguments are. They seem really important at the time and then two years later you can't even remember where it started or what it was about.

RUPERT: It's just sort of growing up. It's natural.

QUESTION: Was it difficult finding a balance and tone in this film?

EMMA: I think that it was quite difficult. I mean, the book has such a huge audience, which are children, and so you get a lot of young kids who are in[to] this, and so part of the people who are making this film feel like we shouldn't make it too scary, because they'll cut out this huge audience who are so passionate and love the Harry Potter films. At the same time, they want to be faithful to the book, which is a darker book; and I think that they did get a really good balance. I do think that it was faithful, and I think that this one is darker and scarier. I think that was the best way to go, because from the very beginning they wanted to stay faithful to what this is about and were not worried about pleasing everyone.

DANIEL: I think that it wouldn't have been as hard for us as for Steve Kloves, who wrote the script. I mean, to do something as massive as the fourth book would be hard. I certainly wouldn't envy that task. He did an amazing job on it. To me, the humor is actually essential to the darkness in a way, because if you have that darkness running through the entire film, by the end you would be tired and it would be completely ineffective. Whereas if you've got the humor, it's easier. What's quite nice is that Mike [Newell] lulls you in. You've got that quite dark opening with the snake and the caretaker being killed, but it then goes into this sort of feel that's like the first film again. It's all wide-eyed and full of wonder and everything, and that highlights

The three stars of the Harry Potter films have grown up before our eyes. (Rex Features/CP Photo)

the fact that suddenly they come out of the tent and everything is ablaze. And you sort of instantly are taken in, and it's more of a shock when you go into that darker world. I do think that the humor is essential to that.

EMMA: I don't think that Mike held us back in any way. He's always really, really pushed us. He's been able to make it really, really real. He really went there. The other thing is that he really treats us as adults. He was expecting us to be professional the whole time; more than before, in some ways.

DANIEL: When we could get away with more, because we were a bit younger.

EMMA: Yeah. And so there were no excuses, and he really pushed all of us, which was nice because it made me feel like I was well challenged.

QUESTION: Daniel, what were the underwater sequences like?

DANIEL: That was amazing. I mean, that was quite hard work and those days I feel like were the ones where I did work, because normally I think that I've got this thing in my mind that work can't be fun. I trained for about six months beforehand and I would go under there and I was sharing someone else's air from their scuba diving tank. So we both sort of had regulators. And they'd say, "Three, two, one . . ." On the three, I would blow out all the air in my lungs and then on the one I would take a very big gulp of air in and then it's sort of how much action can you do with that amount of breath in your body, kind of thing? The hard thing was not just holding your breath, but it was the fact that I wasn't actually allowed to let any of the air out because Harry is supposed to become a fish with gills. I suppose that there's not supposed to be bubbles going around then. I do have to point out that I had the most amazing stunt team backing me up, the people that I trained with for six months and who were down in the tank with me. They were fantastic.

QUESTION: Are you interested in acting beyond *Harry Potter*?

RUPERT: I think that I'm really enjoying this. Doing all these films has been a really good sort of experience. I think that I'd like to do it in the future. I love this job. I'd like to continue. Definitely. It's not a bad job.

EMMA: I definitely don't want *Harry Potter* to be the last thing that I do. Originally what I sort of used to love was being on a stage and sort of reacting to a live audience. So maybe my calling is more in theater. But I don't know. There are so many different things you can do within it that I don't know where I'll end up. I'm definitely looking around and definitely interested.

DANIEL: I just love doing this and I was trying to sort of work out the other day what's the attraction, why do I love it so much. And I have no idea. I mean, the sort of conclusion that I reached was that it was something to do with the idea that maybe it's like a power thing, because you have a character and in many ways it's up to you how that character is perceived by people who are watching the film. Obviously, it's not just up to you in terms of how it's written in the script and the direction as well. So I suppose that's one of the things. I mean, I love doing it. I have a huge passion for acting, but also I'm quite interested in eventually maybe directing or something like that.

It's simply because I've been so inspired by working with Chris Columbus and Alfonso [Cuaron] and now Mike, and having conversations with David Yates who's doing the fifth film, and also talking to Gary Oldman, who directed this film *Nil By Mouth*, which is a fantastic film. But I think that's a long way down the line for me.

QUESTION: Are there parallels between what your characters are going through and what you are? Do you have boys chasing you?

EMMA: I don't know how to answer that, to be honest. Daniel, you're good at those questions. You take it.

DANIEL: Do I have boys chasing after me? [Laughs] To be honest, you talk about parallels in the film, there is a parallel in that both me and Harry are not very good with women. I think I'm better now than I used to be, but I think any man who ever says that he's never had an awkward moment with a girl is a liar. So I think that's probably the main parallel with me and Harry in this film. I would like to say that I got huge amounts of attention, but I think that there's a sort of dividing thing between what people think they're going to get when they see the film and what the reality is. I think that it's slightly grimmer possibly [laughs].

RUPERT: [Laughs] I'm pretty much the same as Danny. I'm probably very close to Ron, really. He's not very lucky.

DANIEL: That's the thing that I quite like about Harry and Ron, they are the worst dates in the world. There were these two cool girls who are played by Afshan [Azad], the girl who plays Padma — she had the misfortune of going out with Ron. She's one of my best friends. I thought that it was just great, because you just feel so sorry for them because this night should be the best night in the world for these girls, but it's horrible and then you have that little bit outside which is quite sort of true with those kinds of dances, those things where you've got sort of the ballroom casualties who are outside weeping, because the night has gone so horribly.

EMMA: Hermione included. That's the thing. I loved doing it so much, because I could relate to so much of what she was going through and I so know that frustration where guys can be so insensitive. I can relate to a lot of things that she experiences and all of her awkward moments, and what that's all about. What's nice about the relationship that she and Victor have, and what Mike really wanted to show, was that Hermione is so insecure about herself and she's never really had any attention from any guy before. So when she sees that they're looking at her it's one of those, "Is that guy really looking at me or am I just crazy?" I mean, he genuinely wanted to come across as she is quite literally being swept off her feet. She doesn't know what is happening to her and she gets caught up in this whirlwind that is this incredibly famous Quidditch player and she can't quite believe that it's happening to her. So it's quite an emotional roller coaster for her.

QUESTION: What's the best part of this process?

DANIEL: Harry Potter is a very gradual process, because it's so huge and you piece it together day by day and it goes through all these different stages. It's fifteen minutes of credits, thousands of people work on it and all that work is [as] important as the rest. And then it amounts to this massive thing at the end of it which is amazing, and it's just a fantastic thing to see, because even if we hadn't . . . I mean, I believe that we've made a great film, a really good film, but even if we hadn't, the sense of achievement would still be this amazing thing. So that would probably be, for me, the thing about this film.

EMMA: You kind of think that after working on something for the five years that I've been doing this, you would start to get bored, the shine would start to wear off and that it might get boring, and that you would get complacent and want to move on. But a couple of weeks back, the trailer was shown for the first time on ITV News and I remember coming into the kitchen and it was on the screen and it said that it was going to play in five minutes. I was literally filled with excitement all over again about the fact that I was part of it and that I was in it. When I saw it, I was literally so excited again. So probably sort of starting to see it all come out, because there's a huge wait. A killer wait. You've worked on the film for eleven months, and then you have to wait six months to see it and it's painful. You just so want to know what it looks like.

RUPERT: I find it hard to actually remember anything, really. It's quite a long time in between. So I would say, yeah, seeing it at the end is the thing. Definitely.

QUESTION: What stands out about this film in terms of your character?

DANIEL: I think that the main theme of the entire film is sort of like a story arc — and I think that it comes across more in this film than it has in the last ones — is that the whole film is about a loss of innocence. If you look at the first one it's all sort of very wide-eyed and almost naive. He's quite naive in thinking, because it's a magical world that it's going to be better than the world that he's come from. Whereas in actual fact, it's not. There are further extremes. It can have extremes of joy, which possibly are more than in the normal human world, but also the depths that people can sink to, in terms of people like Voldemort. I think that in this film he starts to wake up to that fact even more than he did in the last one. I think he comes to the realization that if he's going to make it in life, he's going to be making it alone. I think that's probably the main thing he experiences, that he sort of discovers in this film.

QUESTION: Can you talk about what it's been like working with Mike Newell?

EMMA: It was so nice that he really wanted to hear what we had to say and what we thought, because that might kind of take it to a new level. In a way, I think sometimes it's difficult, and I go, "I can't get this right. Just tell me what you want me to do and how you want this to be, because I'm going crazy." And he'd just say, "I can't tell you how to do it and I'm not going to tell you how to do it. Just think about it." It was nice the way that he guided us really well. We had to take responsibility for ourselves, for our roles, for how we came across. He put a lot of trust in us to do that.

DANIEL: I suppose that's sort of the main thing that I got out of Mike's directing was that we're now old enough to appreciate scenes being analyzed and broken down. The fact is that there is such a rigorous process of drafting the script on a Harry Potter film. The same is true on all films, but on Harry Potter we must go through about seven drafts before we get to the one that we start shooting on. So basically by that time, if it's in the script, it pushes the story forward and it advances things and it is there for a reason. Mike was fantastic about going into detail about things. I remember sort of the first time we were rehearsing with Mike. It was me and Matt Lewis, who plays Neville, who is fantastic. He's just the greatest guy. We were doing the scene, and on the page the scene was around an inch and a half long and we spent about an hour and a quarter rehearsing it and going through different things. We were sort of going, "Right. If this is how long a scene that's an inch and a half long takes, how long will it be when we get to the twelve-page scene with Voldemort?" We were sort of slightly apprehensive about how we were going to be pushed, but it was very exciting. I mean, he realized that we're now old enough to appreciate really going into detail with us about the scenes. I think that was probably the main thing that changed.

RUPERT: It's the same, really. I've finished school now and so it sort of feels like I'm sort of more grown up now anyway. But Mike was great in a sort of brilliant way.

QUESTION: Now that you've played these characters over four films, do you feel a connection to them? And are you excited about doing the rest of the films?

EMMA: I'm hugely attached to Hermione's character, because there's so much of me that goes into her, and so much of my experience. One thing that Mike did was have me kind of regurgitate my own experiences and sort of put them into her.

DANIEL: That's quite disgusting [laughs].

EMMA: [Laughs] Sorry. He made me apply them to what Hermione was going through. I know that if anyone else were to play

Hermione, I wouldn't be able to deal with that. It would kill me. I'm hugely close to her.

DANIEL: That was a good way of putting it. It's not a pretty image, but you're absolutely right in that he did make us draw upon our own experiences. I think that you can't really help but feel attached to your character. I certainly can't help but feel attached to [Harry] in some ways. I don't know about twins. I don't know if me playing him has turned out how I am like him now, or being so close to him over the past five years has influenced my own character. I mean, I don't think that I'm going to develop a complex over it or anything, but it's a sort of slightly interesting thing. I mean, it's very hard to separate yourself from him in some ways, but ultimately you go home at night and it's not like you stay in character all the time. It would be very hard to be a method actor on Harry Potter, because then you'd have to find the figure of ultimate evil somewhere, and they don't exist. So that would be my not-particularly-clear answer to that question.

December 2005

Definitely proving his desire to stretch his acting muscles, Daniel Radcliffe agreed to star in Peter Shaffer's controversial play *Equus*, which would require him to appear on stage in the nude. *Harry Potter* veteran Kenneth Branagh would direct. Some time later his spokesperson Vanessa Davies would note, "It is an extraordinary play, and he's very much looking forward to the role. He is maturing as an actor and beginning to take on new and challenging roles."

On her official Web site, J.K. Rowling expressed her feelings about writing the seventh and final novel in the Harry Potter series. "I contemplate the task with mingled feelings of excitement and dread, because I can't wait to get started. I have been fine-tuning the fine-tuned plan for [book] seven during the past few weeks so I can really set to work in January."

The year ended with actor Robbie Coltrane — better known as Hagrid to Potter fans — being given an OBE (Order of the British Empire).

January 2006

Harry Potter and the Half-Blood Prince was confirmed as the best-selling book of 2005, selling 7.2 million copies.

The film version of *Goblet of Fire* broke all IMAX records in its presentation on those giant-screened theaters.

In an interview with Britain's *Telegraph*, J.K. Rowling discussed Harry and the fact that he was "born" the day her mother died. "I know I was writing *Harry Potter* at the moment my mother died," she reflected, "I never told her about [him]. Barely a day goes by when I do not think of her. There would be so much to tell her; impossibly much." In the same interview, she admitted that she had a hard time dealing with fame, explaining that it was as though she had been living under a rock for such a long period of time and suddenly someone lifted that rock off and began shining a flashlight on her. "I was petrified," she admitted, "and didn't know how to handle it."

Thousands of hopeful teenage girls between 13 and 16 braved the cold in London to try to audition for the part of Luna Lovegood in the fifth film adaptation, *Harry Potter and the Order of the Phoenix*.

Security guard Aaron Lambert was found guilty of having stolen two copies of *The Half-Blood Prince* before its publication date, and threatening a reporter with what turned out to be a fake gun. The sentence was four and a half years in jail. Proclaimed judge Richard Bray, "You realized the books had considerable potential value. It was only through the good services of the press and police

Thousands of teenage girls braved the chilly weather in the hope of securing the role of Luna Lovegood in Order of the Phoenix. *(Sang Tan/AP Photo)*

that fans of Harry Potter — both young and old — were able to read the book without their pleasure being polluted by the premature publication of the plot."

J.K. Rowling announced that she would be visiting Romania to participate in a fundraising event for The Children's High Level Group, which focuses its attention on child health and development in Romania and across Europe.

Casting news for *Order of the Phoenix*: Actor George Harris was brought on for the role of Kingsley Shacklebolt, a Dark Wizard catcher; and Robbie Jarvis as the younger incarnation of Harry's father, James Potter.

Both J.K. Rowling and Daniel Radcliffe were among celebrity guests for Queen Elizabeth's 80th birthday party, a gala devoted strictly to children and the desire to help them explore new worlds and characters through reading.

February 2006

MTV heralded the fact that *Order of the Phoenix* would begin shooting early in the month. In a news story on the network's Web site, the plot was described as follows: "Harry has trouble getting the magical world to believe that evil Lord Voldemort has come back. Only Harry's close friends and a few supporters (including Professor Dumbledore) take the news seriously, but with the Ministry of Magic officially disavowing the boy wizard's claims, it's up to Dumbledore's newly re-formed anti-evil-wizard league, the Order of the Phoenix, to take matters into its own hands. In the same spirit, Harry forms Dumbledore's Army, an underground Defense Against the Dark Arts class."

CBCC Newsround reported on casting for *Order of the Phoenix*: Sian Thomas as Amelia Bones, Head of the Magical Law Enforcement Office; Charles Hughes as Young Wormtail; Susie Shinner as Young Lily Potter, Richard Leaf as Auror Dawlish and Nick Shim as Zacharias Smith. Returning would be the Dursley family, absent from *Goblet of Fire*. Many fans have written fan fiction chronicling the adventures of young James and Lily Potter.

March 2006

Britain's Sony Ericsson Empire Awards, voted on by the British moviegoing public, gave a special award to the Harry Potter films and "their outstanding contribution to the British movie industry." Daniel Radcliffe, Emma Watson and Rupert Grint were there to pick up the award.

Goblet of Fire sold more than nine million copies in its first week of release on DVD.

Prisoner of Azkaban director Alfonso Cuaron was asked by *Entertainment Weekly* if he had any interest in returning to the franchise. "The most beautiful two years of my life were on [*Azkaban*]," he told *EW*. "The attraction of *Harry Potter* — not just the movie franchise, but the J.K. Rowling books — is that it's surrounded by this beneficial energy. So there is a temptation to revisit that. I haven't ruled it out. On the other hand, nobody knows what the last book is going to be."

Fans were overjoyed to learn that a deal was set up for Gary Oldman to return as Sirius Black in *Order of the Phoenix*.

J.K. Rowling was dismayed to discover that she couldn't find pads of paper — her preferred means of writing her novels — in her home city, Edinburgh. "What is a writer who likes to write longhand supposed to do when she hits her stride and then realizes to her horror she has covered every bit of blank paper in her bag? And there's a university here! What do the students use?" she mused on her Web site. Shortly thereafter, she was flooded with paper from fans.

Oxfordshire reported that Emma Watson was participating in Oxford's first International Young Women's Hockey Festival.

J.K. Rowling was awarded the Book of the Year at the British Book Awards for *Harry Potter and the Half-Blood Prince*.

April 2006

J.K. Rowling, who serves as the patron of the Multiple Sclerosis Society Scotland, donated money toward the construction of a $4 million MS research facility. "It is an extremely exciting step forward in the ongoing battle to try to unlock the mysteries of multiple sclerosis," she enthused to IBNLive.

To benefit charity, Daniel Radcliffe paid nearly $50,000 for a handwritten history of Sirius Black's family tree, which was penned by J.K. Rowling. The charity was for Book Aid International, which provides books to schools in Africa.

Harry Potter and the Goblet of Fire became the fifth highest grossing global movie of all time.

May 2006

CBBC Newsround reported that due to her pregnancy, Helen McCrory would *not* be playing Death Eater Bellatrix Lestrange. In her place would be Helena Bonham Carter.

J.K. Rowling wins the Book of the Year at the British Book Awards for Harry Potter and the Half Blood Prince. *(Anthony Harvey/PA/CP Photo)*

June 2006

In a poll within *The Book Magazine*, J.K. Rowling was named greatest British writer.

Author Tom Morris turned to J.K. Rowling's fictional world for lessons on leadership in his book, *If Harry Potter Ran General Electric*.

Daniel Radcliffe, Emma Watson and Rupert Grint were announced as starring in a Harry Potter "scene" written especially for Queen Elizabeth's 80th birthday gala.

Warner Brothers announced that *Harry Potter and the Order of the Phoenix* would be reaching theaters on July 13, 2007.

Interviewed for Reuter's press agency, J.K. Rowling hinted at her feelings writing the final Harry Potter novel. "I am feeling sad as it is the last one," she said. "But so far, so good."

BBC News reported news about characters dying in the seventh Harry novel. "One character got a reprieve," J.K. Rowling said on the *Richard and Judy Show*, "but I have to say two die that I didn't intend to die." The media and the Internet exploded with conjecture that Harry would be one of the two who would perish.

July 2006

Thanks to her efforts for MS research, J.K. Rowling was given an honorary degree from Aberdeen University. "I am extremely honored and thrilled — it's very exciting," the author said.

Goblet of Fire took home two trophies from the 2006 Home Entertainment Awards in Las Vegas in the categories of Best Sell-Through Title and Best DVD Extras.

Sixth Sense and *Lady in the Water* director M. Night Shyamalan expressed potential interest in directing the final Harry Potter film. "I want to see a serious emotional conflict," Night offered to the *Scotsman*, "like if Ron goes to the wrong side. Power has such a double-edged sword. I want the audience to feel that for a moment."

Astrologer Dr. Mark Hammergren, based at Chicago's Adler Planetarium, who discovered asteroid 43844, decided to name it after J.K. Rowling.

If the Harry from year four and the Harry from year seven were ever to meet, the results might be the punk rock band Harry and the Potters, made up of brothers Joe (he's Harry year four) and Paul (Harry year seven) DeGeorge. The duo are joined by drummer Ernie Kim, and all three wear black-rimmed glasses, gray V-neck sweaters and ties. Their music can be checked out on their Web site at www.eskimolabs.com/hp. The Portland, Oregon, brothers' band debuted their punk rock band at restaurant and bookstore performances. Accompanying them was the message that "reading rocks!"

August 2006

Harry fans bid $1,000 a ticket to hear J.K. Rowling do a reading when she came to America to read alongside Stephen King and John Irving in a bid to raise money for two charities — The Haven Foundation, which funds artists who are unable to perform due to a disability or illness, and Doctors Without Borders, an organization that brings emergency aid to people affected by conflict or natural disasters. "For me," Rowling explained, "this was a unique opportunity to raise money for two great, important causes, read to American fans for the first time in six years and get to meet and read alongside Stephen King and John Irving." At the same time, she offered her feelings about what life will be like post-Harry. "I will go through a mourning period, then I will have to think of something else to write."

J.K. Rowling is flanked by authors John Irving and Stephen King at a press conference for a reading they would be doing together. At the press conference, both King and Irving begged Rowling not to kill Harry in the final book. (Seth Wenig/AP Photo)

Other casting news for *Order of the Phoenix*: Natalie Tena as Nymphadora Tonks, Kathryn Hunter as Mrs. Figg and Evanna Lynch as Luna Lovegood. Also announced as composer was director David Yates' frequent collaborator, Nicholas Hooper.

During a press conference while she was in New York, J.K. Rowling offered the following about book seven: "I think some people will love it, and some people will loathe it. I'm well into writing it now. To an extent, the pressure's off, because this is the last book, so I feel quite liberated. It's fun in a way that it hasn't been before, because I'm finally doing my resolution. There's still a lot to find out and expand on, and I will probably leave some loose ends, but there won't be a book eight. I've plotted the series out and I'd run out of plot if I pushed it past there."

Katie Leung, who plays Cho Chang in both *Goblet of Fire* and *Order of the Phoenix*, was cast to play a Chinese warrior in the film *Mulan* (not related to the Disney animated film of the same name).

September 2006

In the wake of the British terrorist threat, no carry-on luggage was allowed, and U.S. airport security attempted to stop J.K. Rowling from carrying her mostly handwritten manuscript for book seven — and the only copy of it — on board with her. Rowling simply refused to part with it and in the end they elected to allow her to hold on to it. "I don't know what I would have done if they hadn't," she mused. "Sailed home, probably."

As the *Evening Standard* reported, Rupert Grint admitted he was having a hard time preparing for his driver's test. When asked how things were going, he said, "Not that well. I've had a few more [lessons], so I suppose I'm pretty much ready for my next test."

Celebrity Spider reported that in an online poll, Lord Voldemort was deemed the top villain among children, ahead of such luminaries as Sauron from *The Lord of the Rings*, Mrs. Coulter from *His Dark Materials*, Superman's arch-enemy Lex Luthor and Batman's foe, the Joker.

J.K. Rowling dismissed claims that she was almost finished with book seven. "I haven't written 750 pages of book seven," she said, "and if I had, I'd be very worried, as I'm not close to finishing it yet."

Fans were delighted to discover that a few shots from *Harry Potter and the Order of the Phoenix* were being released online, particularly one shot in which Harry, on the ground, is trying to ward off Dementors.

In a *Newsweek* interview, Emma Watson sang the praises of *Order of the Phoenix* director David Yates. "David won't settle for anything that looks like acting," she laughs. "What keeps coming up a lot is his search for truth in the characters and the performances. He really wants it to be real. The fourth film was sort of about all the tasks, fighting dragons and all of that. This film is about Harry fighting his inner demons more than dragons. It's about the emotional journey. So I think David is the perfect director for that."

October 2006

A granite plaque was place on a building important in Harry Potter's history. "J.K. Rowling wrote some of the early chapters of *Harry Potter* in the rooms on the first floor of this building," reads the plaque, which is placed next to a photo of Rowling outside the Black Medicine Coffee Company shop.

Warner Brothers announced that the first trailer for *Order of the Phoenix* would be attached to the theatrical release of the CG penguin film, *Happy Feet*.

A first edition signed Harry Potter novel raised over $100,000 for a children's charity in auction.

In an online interview as reported by canmag.com, Rupert Grint suggested there was a chance that *Sorcerer's Stone* and *Chamber of Secrets* director Chris Columbus might return for film six or seven.

While it won't actually make people invisible as Harry's does, a team of American and British scientists developed an "invisibility cloak" that will render people, tanks and ships invisible to radar.

With Daniel Radcliffe worth an approximate $35–40 million, *Newsweek* asked if he was concerned about girls seeking him out for his money. "They are always a worry," he said, "but I've got pretty good instincts for people. Normally, the people who are not genuine are the ones who say, 'You know, I'm not just being your friend because you're Harry Potter, right?' And it's like, 'Oh, fine, but if that's the case, why do you need to say that?'"

November 2006

As reported by the *Colgate University News*, wizards and muggles of all ages took part in a reading of the first Harry Potter novel, *The Sorcerer's Stone*, at the Hamilton Public Library. "One parent," they offered, "dressed as Professor Snape, read a chapter in full character, British accent and all, much to the delight of listeners of all ages. Many children, dressed in their wizard robes, the typical attire of a Hogwarts student, enjoyed the arts and crafts area where they could create their own Harry Potter glasses or make theme-inspired buttons."

On her official Web site, J.K. Rowling teased her fans with vague mentions of the title for book seven. "I've now got a third title," she wrote. "I've been thinking back and I've had more titles than this for a couple of the previous books, so I'm not too worried by this. Title three currently is ahead by a short nose, or perhaps that should be a vowel and two consonants."

Controversy continued to arise over the notion that Daniel Radcliffe would be appearing nude in the West End production of *Equus*. Producer David Push noted to the *Sunday Telegraph*, "The nudity and those scenes are an essential part of the story. We are not doing it as an excuse to show Harry Potter's willy. Daniel is fully committed to the role and he has not asked for any special favors . . . I have been wanting to do a production of *Equus* for eight years and the problem has always been finding the right boy. When Daniel performed for us at the workshop, we couldn't take our eyes off him."

J.K. Rowling won a legal ruling over Iranian cybersquatters who had registered the domain www.JKRowling.ir.

The *Daily Record* reported on the shooting of Daniel's kissing scene with actress Katie Leung, who reprises her role of Cho Chang in *Order of the Phoenix*. Smiled Daniel, "We probably got it on the thirtieth take. My God, it was fun. Me and Katie, we were awkward and nervous — at first, but once we got it, it was fine."

EA Games announced a new title that would tie into the fifth Harry Potter film. Said Senior VP Warner Brothers Interactive Entertainment Jason Hall, "Working with EA, we look forward to offering fans the most authentic Harry Potter game to date; one which captures the compelling story of the fiction and high visual quality of the movie. After reading the book and seeing the film, fans will be able to take advantage of the complete interactive experience with the *Harry Potter and the Order of the Phoenix* game."

Harry Potter and the Goblet of Fire won a British BAFTA Award in the category of the BAFTA Kids' Vote. Rupert Grint attended the ceremony.

December 2006

Covering *Order of the Phoenix*, *USA Today* featured an interview with Daniel Radcliffe in which he discussed the film: "Harry is waking up to the fact that life is very hard and people can be very nasty to each other and can do terrible things. There's this ongoing theme which runs through the whole series, and that's a loss of innocence."

Speaking to Australia's *Herald Sun*, Daniel Radcliffe admitted that he was a little nervous about how his part in this August's *December Boys* will be received. Set in 1960s Australia, the film is about four orphans who compete with each other to prove who is more adoptable. Noted Daniel, "It does feel like a big deal and I am nervous about how it's going to be received, and I'm nervous about what people are going to say, but that's what happens. I think people will like it and the one thing they genuinely can't say is that I'm playing Harry."

In an interview with *Newsweek*, director David Yates emphasized the importance of the performances in the film. "The most important thing on screen is the actors," he noted. "If the performance isn't real, that million-dollar special effects shot behind the actor doesn't count for anything."

J.K. Rowling told Sky News that the challenge of finishing book seven was so stressful that it was affecting her dreams. "I don't think anyone who has not been in a similar situation can possibly know how this feels. I am alternately elated and overwrought. For years now, people have asked me if I ever dream I am in Harry's world. The answer was no until a few nights ago when I had an epic dream that I was Harry and the narrator."

The Internet went wild on December 21 when J.K. Rowling announced on her Web site that the official title of book number seven — the last Harry Potter novel ever — would be *Harry Potter and the Deathly Hallows*, and that two characters would die. Speculation began running high that those two characters would ultimately be Harry and Voldemort.

January 2007

After J.K. Rowling announced the title of her seventh and final Harry Potter novel, there was much conjecture about what exactly it meant, with fear creeping in that it could signal the death of Harry himself. The *Columbus Dispatch* turned to Scholastic for an explanation, and the publisher's Kristen Moran replied that people in the office rushed to an unabridged dictionary. "Hallows means holy person or saint," said Moran. "But we really don't know what the title means." That report also quoted Rowling from her site, where she wrote that she wasn't finished with the book yet. "I'm now writing scenes that have been planned, in some cases, for a dozen years or even more," Rowling is quoted. "I both want and don't want to finish this book (don't worry, I will)."

Years earlier, after Rowling had been turned down by numerous publishers and literary agencies, Christopher Little of his self-named agency took the author on as a client and the rest, of course, is a bit of magical history. Now the Christopher Little Literary Agency is offering a £1,500 prize and a chance for representation to students who were taking a creative writing course at London's City University. One point they made is that they're not looking for a Rowling clone.

Britain's *The Mirror* reported, "The final Harry Potter tale is No. 1 in Amazon's online book chart — even though a release date has not been set. *Harry Potter and the Deathly Hallows* topped the list just eight hours after customers were offered the chance to reserve a copy online."

In an amazing turn of events, 23-year-old Chilean journalism student Francisca Solar, who had written an unofficial Harry Potter story, *Harry Potter and the Decline of the High Elves*, found herself signed to a three-book deal by Random House. The first book in the series will be called *The Seventh M.*

According to *The Daily Princetonian*, Daniel Radcliffe would be joining the university as a part of the class of 2011. "Rumors have swirled for months that Radcliffe, who will graduate this June from the City of London School, was considering Princeton," stated the *Princetonian*.

According to the BBC, thousands of copies of J.K. Rowling's *Fantastic Beasts* and *Quidditch Through the Ages* that were intended for recycling were stolen and now the fear is that these books, the proceeds for which all went to charity, will now be sold for profit.

Inspired by the Harry Potter phenomenon, the BBC announced a reality series called *The Sorcerer's Apprentice*, which will follow a group of children who are learning magic at a Harry Potter–like boarding school. The kids will learn card tricks, Latin spells and illusions.

Photos of Daniel Radcliffe nearly nude from the London stage production of *Equus* made their way into the media. The ensuing reports and outcry from some outraged parents was immediate. With Harry Potter headlines filling magazines, newspapers and TV news shows, it perhaps reinforces the reason why Daniel wanted to do the play in the first place: to create an image of himself separate and apart from the boy wizard.

February 2007

Ten years after it began, it comes to a close as J.K. Rowling announced that her final Harry Potter novel, *Harry Potter and the Deathly Hallows* would be published on July 21, 2007, just a week after the fifth film adaptation, *Order of the Phoenix*, reaches theaters. In some ways it feels like the end of an era, but in another, it's just the beginning. Fans will have two additional films to look forward to, and in all likelihood J.K. Rowling has secured herself a place in literary history; her work undoubtedly destined to live on for generations to come. Words to commemorate what she has given all of us could never suffice, so perhaps it is best to be succinct but heartfelt: Thank you.